Penguin Handbooks
Portuguese Cookery

D0766412

Ursula Bourne was born in 1921 and educated in
England, Switzerland and France. During the war
she served as a V.A.D. in the British Red Cross and
afterwards worked with the British Council and
the London Red Cross. After their marriage she
and her husband took up fruit farming in Suffolk
where they lived until 1963 when they moved to a
village near Colchester. Her other interests include
glass engraving, painting and (with her husband)
glove puppets. She has two children, a son and a
daughter.

Ursula Bourne

Portuguese Cookery

Illustrated by Alastair Heseltine

Penguin Books

Penguin Books Ltd, Harmondsworth,
Middlesex, England
Penguin Books Inc., 7110 Ambassador Road,
Baltimore, Maryland 21207, U.S.A.
Penguin Books Australia Ltd, Ringwood,
Victoria, Australia

First published 1973
Reprinted 1973

Copyright © Ursula Bourne, 1973

Made and printed in Great Britain by
Cox & Wyman Ltd, London, Reading and Fakenham
Set in Monotype Times

To G. C. B.

Without whose encouragement, criticism and tasting, this book would never have been written.

Contents

Acknowledgements

For help in collecting material for this book, I would
like to thank the Tourist Office in Lisbon, particularly
Senhora Alice Alvarez; Senhora María de Lourdes
Modesto, of Lisbon, the well-known authority on food;
Senhor Daniel Constant of Oporto, writer, artist and
gourmet, who was so patient over my numerous
questions; and the Casa de Portugal in London,
particularly Senhora Camara.   U. B.

Introduction

Portuguese cookery is distinctive and varied. It is unlike any other European cuisine, even the Spanish, which it might be expected to resemble because of the close proximity of the two countries.

Though Portugal is a small country it is one of many contrasts in landscape, climate and character of the people. The cooking is generally simple, using the good local produce, but the Portuguese enjoy cooking and eating well. I have written this book to introduce Portuguese dishes to cooks in this country, rather than to tell them what to eat in Portugal. However, I think it may be of interest as a background to the cuisine to give a short description of the different parts of the country.

In the north-east, running up to the Spanish border, lies the Trás-os-Montes, which means 'Beyond the Mountains'. It is a descriptive name, as the mountains cut off this region from the rest of Portugal. In the valley of the upper Douro grapes are grown on terraces cut out of the rocky slopes; but on the higher ground the country is wild and harsh and, except where forests have been planted, the vegetation is mainly of scrub and heath.

The people need to be tough to withstand the bitter winters and bleak conditions. They are said to be akin to the Celts and certainly to the people of Galicia in Spain. Like the Celts, they are a superstitious people and many of their religious customs date back to very early days. It is surprising that they are able to make a living off such country, but some of the finest herds of pigs are reared in this region and it is famous for all manner of sausages, as well as pork in every form.

West of the Trás-os-Montes is the Minho, and, though it is on almost the same latitude, it is very different. It has the highest rainfall in Portugal, and consequently the countryside is green and very beautiful. There is an abundance of fruits and vegetables, and many kinds of fish are caught in the rivers and off the coast. From this area also come the *vinhos verdes*, young and slightly sparkling wines which are a suitable accompaniment to the rather rich food. The people are gay and light-hearted, and during the annual festivals there seems to be almost continuous music and dancing. The most important festival of the region takes place at Viana do Castelo during the month of August, and people come from far and wide to visit it. Each morning starts with a salvo of rockets and each evening there is a magnificent display of fireworks from the bridge over the river. During the day there are many processions, the men, women and children dressed in the colourful regional costumes and carrying on their heads large baskets of fruits, cakes, bread and even bottles of wine.

South of the Minho is the region of the Douro Litoral, in which is the important and busy city of Oporto. Well known for the port wine trade, it is also known as a place where good food is taken seriously. In the city there are a number of small, comfortable eating places, which seem to be almost entirely patronized by men. In one where we had lunch I found myself to be the only woman and felt a little strange. It was interesting to watch with what care and real enjoyment the menu was studied and discussed with the waiter.

Between Oporto and Lisbon are three regions, Beira Litoral, the Ribatejo, and Estremadura.

The coast of Beira Litoral has become rather popular with holiday makers, but there are still a number of small, unspoilt fishing villages. The town of Aveiro is at the head of a lagoon formed by a spit of sand twelve miles long, and travelling along this sand strip one feels almost in another world. It is a place of dunes, stunted trees and sea birds, and on the peaceful waters of the lagoon are the curiously shaped boats of the seaweed gatherers. Not far inland is Coimbra, the university city; and near by, in the Bairrada area, the speciality is *leitão assado*, sucking pig roasted on a spit – tender, succulent, with a slightly sharp taste of vinegar and pepper.

The Ribatejo is the cattle-breeding region, where cattle are reared not only for beef but also for the bullring. It is peaceful, rolling countryside, where the colourful costumes of the *campinos*, the horsemen who tend the cattle, can still be seen.

Estramadura is a prosperous farming and horticultural region, with a lovely stretch of coastline running down to Lisbon and beyond. This part of the coast is famous for its lobsters and both Peniche, on the coast, and the Berlenga Islands have their own ways of cooking them. Inland, grain is grown, as well as many fruits and vegetables. The vineyards of Colares, near Sintra, are planted on sandy slopes facing the Atlantic, protected from the fierce gales only by a type of wattle hurdle.

Each small town and village seems to have its own speciality and while sampling some of these there are many places of interest to visit: the impressive and historical monasteries of Batalha and Alcobaça, the many individual and charming fishing villages and the completely walled medieval town of Óbidos, where the narrow streets of little white houses are a riot of colour with flowers and hanging plants. It is a region where one can wander happily for many days.

Lisbon is in Estramadura. As it is the capital, food from all the different regions can be found there and a number of restaurants specialize in regional foods. However, it has some dishes all of its own, notably *iscas*, which is liver marinated in wine, vinegar and spices.

Lisbon has a charm all of its own, from the old quarter of Alfama, which was one of the few places untouched by the great earthquake of 1755, to the busy waterfront on the River Tagus and to the new parts of the city. It is not large and can be happily explored on foot; but if this idea is daunting the taxis are numerous and cheap and the trams and buses still cheaper and also entertaining. It is said that May and June are the months in which to visit the capital, when the jacaranda trees are in bloom and everything is fresh and green; but I find Lisbon charming and exhilarating whatever the time of year.

In Lisbon one should try to visit at night one of the restaurants or cafés at which Fado can be heard. The pathos and charm of these songs are indescribable and, though they are now well known in this country, I think they can only really be appreciated when heard 'live'. If the singer is a woman, she almost always has a black shawl draped round her head; this is sometimes said to be in memory of Maria Severa, a famous *fadista* of earlier days, who came to a sad end at the age of 26 from eating too many roasted pigeons. The singer is usually accompanied by two guitars: all the notes of the tune are played on a Portuguese guitar, the accompaniment on a Spanish guitar. During the performance the atmosphere is tense, hardly a sound except from the performers; and it is the depth of bad manners to talk during the singing.

Just south of Lisbon between the estuaries of the rivers Tagus and Sado is the Arrábida. This also is in Estramadura, but it is a distinctive area which needs a few lines to itself. It is named after the range of mountains running along the promontory from east to west, and, while not large, is extremely beautiful. On both the northern and southern slopes of the mountains grow all manner of wild flowers, including the charming hoop-petticoat daffodils.

Near the south-western point is Sesimbra, which, though it is a popular holiday resort, is first and foremost a thriving fishing village. Many different kinds of fish are caught off this part of the coast, including red mullet, sardines, tunny and swordfish, for which it is famous.

On the coast between Sesimbra and Setúbal are a number of beautiful bays and inlets, which are popular with Lisboans during the week-end; and from the mountainous road there are magnificent views of the coast and of the Troia peninsular. This was the site of a large Roman town which was engulfed by a tidal wave. Now it is just a long sandbank, but remains of the town can still be found.

Setúbal is famed for oranges and for fish, particularly red mullet, the town's speciality being *salmonetes grealhados à Setúbalense*. Oranges are used in many ways, from *doce de larange* to conserves and preserves.

Continuing south, the Alentejo, the largest of all the regions, is a wide expanse of sun-scorched and arid earth, which seems to support little except the cork tree and the olive. In this countryside, the dark brown naked trunks of the cork trees, stripped of their bark, contrast with the lighter brown of the soil; and against this stand out the olive trees, resembling wizened old men, grey and gnarled. However, in the east of the region, before the land becomes dried up by the fierce summer sun, a great deal of wheat is grown; and the Alentejo bread is well known and is used in a number of dishes of the region. There are fine herds of pigs, and game of all kinds is abundant. The regional diet is generally heavy and filling. This is largely from necessity, as the people of the Alentejo are poor. The dishes are rather unusual, some with a curious mixture of ingredients, the most notable possibly being pork with clams.

The Algarve, in the extreme south, is shut off from the rest of Portugal by the Monchique mountains, which form both a climatic and a scenic barrier. Once over the mountains the sun seems to beat down more fiercely, the buildings are Moorish in style and the vegetation almost tropical. It is a land of sunshine and magnificent beaches and of small towns and villages which remain attractive in spite of their development as tourist resorts.

The region is famed gastronomically above all else for its rich cakes and sweetmeats, many of which are thought to be of Arab origin. It produces many kinds of fruit and vegetables and a great variety of excellent fish, from sardine and tunny to octopus and squid. It is a land of plenty as well as of beauty and sunshine.

The part of Portugal I have left to the last, possibly because it is my favourite, is made up of two regions, Beira Baixa and Beira Alta. Bordered by the Douro in the north, the Tagus in the south and the Spanish border in the east, and containing the Serra da Estrela, the highest range of mountains in Portugal, the whole area forms an entity and is still quite unspoilt; for this reason it seems to me to be more Portuguese. I am sure that the people of the other regions will heartily disagree with this statement, but I still feel it very strongly.

One of the most charming and graceful towns in Portugal is Viseu, the capital of Beira Alta, set in an attractive wooded countryside. In this neighbourhood also are the vineyards where the famous Dão wines are produced, some of the best in Portugal. Further south, the Serra da Estrela and the neighbourhood of Castelo Branco are well known for their cheeses.

Many of the recipes in this book are, as their titles suggest, specialities of the regions I have described. However, I have not grouped them by regions but according to their place in a meal – soup, fish, and so on – because, as I said at the beginning, this book is intended for the cook rather than for the traveller. So I wish you good cooking and *bon apetit*.

Some Ingredients and Flavours

There are a number of ingredients and flavours either wholly Portuguese or used extensively in Portuguese cookery. As they are included in many of the recipes I thought it would be helpful to describe them more fully.

Bacalhau is dried salted cod. It has, however, a quite distinctive flavour. This true *bacalhau* can be obtained in this country, but unfortunately some shops sell a salted cod in plastic bags which is not *bacalhau* and does not even taste like it. *Bacalhau* needs no plastic bag: it should be in large pieces, dry and hard, and is frequently cut with a saw. In Portuguese grocers' shops it is usually strung up from the roof. It is said that in Portugal there are 365 ways of cooking *bacalhau*, one for each day of the year. Whether this is true or not, there are certainly very many *bacalhau* dishes. Before it is cooked, it must be soaked for at least 24 hours (48 hours is better) in several changes of water. This is to remove the large amount of salt. After that it needs slow, careful simmering.

Squid, which is eaten a great deal in Portugal, is rather rare in this country, but it can be bought from some fishmongers. Do not be put off by its appearance. When carefully cooked it is delicious.

CURED PORK AND SAUSAGES

As I have said in another part of this book, various kinds of cured pork and sausages play an important part in Portuguese cooking. Many of them are not obtainable in this country, and so I have tried to suggest substitutes as near to the originals as possible.

Morcela. A spiced blood sausage made from pork; in some regions, particularly Beira Alta, it contains cumin. A black pudding may be used instead; I often add a little cumin.

Touchinho. Belly of pork. Fat pork or bacon sliced thinly is a good substitute.

Chouriço. A sausage flavoured with paprika and garlic, similar to the Spanish *chorizo*, which can occasionally be obtained in this country. In its place I have suggested using garlic sausage.

Linguiça. Like *chouriço* but made with finer meat. In Portugal it is sometimes burnt in brandy and eaten with bread.

Mortadela. A garlic sausage. Use Italian mortadella.

Paio. Smoked ham sausage flavoured with sweet paprika.

Presunto. Smoked ham similar to a Parma ham.

Salpicão. Smoked, spiced pork.

FLAVOURINGS

Piri-Piri. A seasoning made from small dried red chillies and olive oil, frequently used in Portuguese cooking. It is called *piri-piri* in Brazil, but in Portuguese Africa it is known by the name of *jindungo*. It is quite easy to make and to store, and I give a recipe below. However, Tabasco sauce can be used equally well.

Use a small glass bottle with a glass stopper, which must be airtight. Fill about a third of the bottle with dried chillies and fill to the top with olive oil. Close the bottle tightly and leave for one month before using.

Cumin. A spice which is used in certain regional dishes, particularly those of the Beira Alta. It is easily obtainable here.

Cinnamon. The Portuguese make much use of this spice in their sweets and cakes, both as a flavouring and for decoration.

Coriander. Both the leaves and the seeds of this herb are used. The fresh herb can be bought from some greengrocers in this country and is also easily grown from seed.

A Note on Port

Britain has had a long association with Portugal, particularly through the trade in port wine. The trade began when the ships of the Second Crusade, bound from England to the Middle East, were forced by a gale in the Bay of Biscay to take shelter at Oporto. The Crusaders were persuaded to help the Portuguese king to drive the Moors out of Portugal instead of proceeding to the Middle East and fighting the infidel there. However, it was not until 1386, after the battle of Aljubarrota, in which the English and Portuguese together succeeded in defeating Dom Juan of Castile, who claimed the Portuguese throne, that a treaty of alliance was concluded between the two countries. This treaty, known as the Treaty of Windsor, gave the English freedom to travel throughout Portugal and the right to trade.

During the wars with France, trade between England and Portugal increased: the wines from France and Spain were replaced by wines from Portugal, and in return England traded her cloth. These early Portuguese wines came from the Minho and were exported from the port of Viana do Castelo. They were thin and sharp and were known as Red Portugal. Later, at the end of the Civil War in England, many Royalists fled to Portugal and caused a great amount of ill feeling between that country and the Commonwealth. In consequence the Portuguese king, who badly needed England's support, made a treaty with the Commonwealth in 1654 which gave special privileges to English merchants, including freedom from any new taxes or increases in customs duties, and the right to hold Protestant services. This was the beginning of the large English colony in Lisbon and, especially, in Oporto.

Soon after this, because of the quarrels and almost continuous war between England and France, claret, which previously had been the popular drink in England, was once again replaced by wines from Portugal. The demand was so great that new vineyards were planted on the steep hillsides of the river Douro. The soil here, to all appearances unproductive, was found to be ideally suited to the growing of vines; and because of the difficulty of transport over the mountains the wine was shipped down the river Douro to Oporto instead of down the river Lima to Viano do Castelo. The production of these Douro wines was to a large extent started and encouraged by the English shippers; and these early pioneers of the port trade braved many hardships, including dirty inns, bad food and the hazards of travel on the river Douro, with its dangerous rapids.

It was about this time that brandy began to be added to the wines before shipment, to make them better able to travel. The addition of brandy during fermentation probably started in the eighteenth century, but it was not until the nineteenth that fortification, that is the addition of brandy to arrest fermentation, became general. Meanwhile, during the eighteenth century, to cater for the English taste for rich, dark wines, growers began to introduce sugar, elderberry and strong Spanish wines. The English shippers objected to this adulteration, and in 1755, taking advantage of a depression in the trade, refused to buy any wine. Unfortunately their methods of refusal were very high-handed, and the Portuguese growers, who were in despair at the loss of their livelihood, sent a deputation to Lisbon to the powerful Marquis of

Pombal, prime minister, indeed virtually dictator of Portugal. He had never been in sympathy with the arrogant English shippers, and he now saw his chance to curtail their powers. In 1756 he formed a State Control Company and decreed that all wine for export should be bought at a controlled price. This was really the end of England's total control of the port trade, and though to this day the English still have a great deal of interest in it, it is in conjunction with the Portuguese.

In 1780 the company undertook the clearing of the notorious rapids of the Cachão de Valeira and opened up the countryside of the Alto Douro, which subsequently produced some of the finest wines. It was about this time, too, that the long-necked bottle began to replace the squat jug-like type. These new bottles could be stored on their sides in bins and thus made possible the maturing of vintage wines in bottle, instead of in cask.

The nineteenth century, which includes so many famous vintage years, was the finest for the trade, in spite of numerous setbacks such as war with the French, the siege of Oporto during the Miguelite War and finally, in 1868, the appearance of phylloxera, which ravaged the vineyards for two years and necessitated the introduction of American stock.

The taste for port continued in this country well into the twentieth century and was diminished only in about 1929 when the craze for sherry and cocktail parties began. This blow to the trade was, however, offset by the Americans and French developing a taste for port; and France now drinks 40 per cent of all the port that is sold. The Portuguese have also begun to drink their own port wine, and Portugal is now the biggest market for a new aperitif, the dry, white port.

England is still the biggest importer of vintage port, taking some 90 per cent of all that is sold; but vintage port, which is wine of a particular year, matured in bottle after two years in cask, constitutes only a very small proportion of the port sold. Most is blended and matured in cask. The wine from red grapes has a full red colour initially, but as it ages the colour fades, giving successively what are known as ruby, tawny and light tawny ports. White port is made from white grapes and also tends to become tawny in colour with age. The sweetness of the wine is regulated by the time at which the brandy is added to arrest fermentation.

The wine lodges to which the wines are brought from the vine-yards to mature in the casks are not in Oporto itself, but in Vila Nova de Gaia, which lies on the other side of the river Douro, looking across to one of the oldest districts of Oporto. In the early days of the trade the wine was brought down the river in boats known as *rebelos*. These, with their wide sails and high prows, are often depicted in pictures and posters of Portugal, but now, unfortunately, are few in number. They were superseded first by the railway and then by a road which connects the vineyards with Vila Nova de Gaia. Today the wine is brought down in huge tankers, which look very out of place in the eighteenth-century town, whose narrow streets are more suited to ox-drawn traffic.

Although the Portuguese use wine in many of their dishes, they do not use port as much as we, who associate it so much with the country, might expect. I have, however, included several recipes in which port is used. Some of these were given me by a Portuguese friend who works in one of the port lodges of Vila Nova de Gaia.

Soup

Soup is generally served at both the mid-day and the evening meal. The soup which is eaten throughout Portugal is the *caldo verde*, made from finely shredded cabbage. It can be very good, but it is unfortunate that it is encountered so often, for even something good can pall after a time. However, no book of Portuguese cookery would be complete without it.

In the poorer regions of the country soup is sometimes the main dish of the meal. In the Alentejo, particularly in the southern half, the countryside is parched and arid for much of the time. Beja, the second town of the region, is reputed to be the hottest in Portugal, the temperature often reaching 100° F. The people mostly live off the land, and have a struggle to make anything grow, with the exception of the olive tree, which seems to be able to withstand any amount of drought, and of wheat, from which the Alentejo bread is made. This firm and close-grained bread made from the whole wheat is nearly always an ingredient of an Alentejo soup. It is usually placed in the bottom of the soup tureen and then the liquid is poured over it. A poached or raw egg is occasionally floated on the top. The soggy bread might not be to everyone's taste, so in some recipes I suggest fried croûtons as an alternative. One name for these soups containing bread is *açorda*. The Alentejo bread and garlic soup is both simple and satisfying. It may take a little time to appreciate, but, as with *bacalhau*, once the taste is acquired it is always enjoyed.

Gaspacho is generally thought to be a Spanish dish, but the Portuguese have their own version using Alentejo bread, the smoked pork called *paio* and sometimes sweet marjoram or other herbs.

Soups are also made from various kinds of fish and shell fish and from many vegetables, such as tomatoes, watercress and beans, both fresh and dried.

Caldo verde

In Portugal *caldo verde* is made from the leaves of a very large cabbage known as *couve*. The stalks and any tough parts are removed and the rest is shredded to almost a grass-like fineness. The firm, round cabbages grown in this country are suitable for *caldo verde*, but whatever kind is used *must* be finely shredded, as it is hardly cooked at all.

Serves four

3 medium potatoes	½ lb. cabbage, finely shredded
1½ pints water	seasoning
2 tablespoons olive oil	

Cook the potatoes in the water with a teaspoonful of salt. Remove, mash and return to the water, along with the oil and cabbage. Boil, uncovered, for 3 minutes. Season to taste.

Açorda Alentejana
(Alentejo Bread and Garlic Soup)

Serves four

3 cloves garlic
1 teaspoon salt
4 fl. oz. olive oil
3 tablespoons fresh coriander, chopped

1 pint boiling water
4 slices wholemeal bread
4 poached eggs

Crush the garlic and mix with the salt at the bottom of a soup tureen or bowl. Add the olive oil and the coriander, pour in the water and stir. In each soup-plate put a slice of bread, pour the soup over it and top with a poached egg.

Gaspacho à Alentejana

Serves four

1 green pepper
4 large tomatoes
2 cloves garlic, crushed
2 fl. oz. vinegar
2 fl. oz. olive oil
seasoning
½ pint iced water

sweet marjoram, chopped
¼ lb. *paio* (see p. 18) *or* smoked ham sausage, shredded
½ cucumber, diced
3 oz. fried or toasted bread cubes

Remove the seeds and pith from the pepper. Chop the pepper and tomatoes, and blend in a liquidizer with the garlic, vinegar, oil and seasoning. Add the water and mix well. Chill.

Serve in individual soup bowls with the sweet marjoram, sausage, cucumber and bread cubes sprinkled on top.

Sopa de ervas à Portuguesa
(Portuguese Vegetable Soup)

This is a favourite soup throughout Portugal. It is made with any leaf vegetable, such as cabbage, turnip tops, sorrel, spinach or lettuce. In this recipe I use sprouting broccoli.

Serves four

olive oil
1 medium onion, sliced
¾ pint chicken stock
a purée made from ½ lb.
   potatoes

¾ lb. sprouting broccoli, finely
   chopped
seasoning
2 oz. bread cubes

Heat 3 fl. oz. olive oil in a large saucepan, add the onion and cook gently until it is limp and golden. Pour in the stock, thicken by adding the potato purée and finally put in the broccoli. Season, cover and cook gently until tender.

Meanwhile, brown the bread cubes lightly all over in a little oil in a small frying pan.

Serve the soup very hot, sprinkled with the bread cubes.

Sopa de cebola
(Onion Soup)

Serves four

1½ oz. fat bacon, chopped
olive oil
¼ lb. onions, sliced
1½ pints chicken stock

1 dessertspoon vinegar
salt
4 eggs
2½ oz. bread cubes

Cook the bacon in a saucepan over gentle heat until the fat runs. Add 1½ fl. oz. olive oil and the onions, and cook until the onions are limp and golden. Pour in the stock, season to taste, cover, and simmer for 10 minutes.

Meanwhile fill a large frying pan with water to a depth of about an inch, add the vinegar and a little salt, and bring to the boil. Break each egg separately into a cup and slip them one by one into the gently boiling water. Cook for 3 minutes.

Brown the bread cubes lightly in a little oil.

To serve, lift out the eggs carefully with a perforated spoon, place one in the bottom of each soup plate, and pour the soup over. Lastly, add the fried bread cubes.

Sopa de agriões
(Watercress Soup)

Serves six

2 handfuls watercress
1 lb. potatoes
1½ pints water

milk or chicken stock
2 tablespoons butter

Discard any discoloured leaves of watercress, wash well and drain. Peel the potatoes and cut into smallish pieces. Cook the potatoes and one handful of watercress in the water until the potatoes are tender, about 10 minutes. Make a purée by pressing the mixture through a hair sieve (or in a liquidizer), then add enough milk or chicken stock to make the purée into a thick soup. Bring to the boil again, add the butter and the rest of the watercress, chopped finely, and boil for 3 minutes. Serve at once.

Sopa de feijão frade
(Haricot Bean Soup)

Serves four

¾ lb. haricot or black-eyed
   beans
4 cloves garlic
1 dessertspoon parsley,
   chopped
1 handful mint, chopped

1 tablespoon olive oil
1½ pints chicken broth or
   broth from a *cozido*
   (see p. 56)
seasoning
croûtons of fried bread

Soak the beans overnight, then put them in a saucepan with plenty of water and simmer until tender, about 30 minutes. Drain.

In a large soup tureen crush the garlic, and add the beans, parsley, mint and olive oil.

Heat the broth and pour it over the contents of the tureen. Season to taste, and serve with fried croûtons.

Sopa de tomate à Alentejana

(Tomato Soup in the Alentejo Style)

Serves up to six

5 oz. fat bacon, chopped	1 bay leaf
5 oz. *linguiça* (see p. 18) *or* garlic sausage, sliced	1¾ pints water seasoning
1 large onion, sliced	1 green pepper, sliced
1 lb. tomatoes, skinned, seeded and chopped	stale bread or croûtons

Cook the bacon in a saucepan over low heat until the fat runs. Put in the *linguiça* or garlic sausage and the onion and cook until the onion is soft. Stir in the tomatoes and simmer for 5 minutes. Add the bay leaf, water and seasoning and bring to the boil. Remove the bay leaf and put in the slices of green pepper.

Place a slice of bread in each soup bowl and pour the soup over it. However, if preferred the bread can be cut into cubes, fried in a little oil and scattered over the soup.

Crême de favas

(Bean Soup)

Serves four

1 lb. shelled broad beans	seasoning
1 pint chicken stock	croûtons of fried bread
a little olive oil	

Skin the beans and cook them in the stock until tender. Sieve or liquidize, add a very little oil and adjust the seasoning. Serve with the croûtons.

Sopa de camarões

(Prawn Soup)

In Portugal fresh prawns are used in this recipe and cooking them is part of the process. They are not readily available in this country so in the recipe given below I have used cooked prawns and gently simmered the shells and heads to make the necessary fish stock.

Serves four

8 oz. prawns	2 tablespoons flour
¾ pint water	1 glass dry white wine
2 oz. butter	4 egg yolks
1 onion, finely sliced	4 tablespoons cream
2 large carrots, grated	seasoning
1 sprig parsley, chopped	

Shell the prawns and put the shells, heads and tails in a saucepan with the water, cover, bring to the boil and simmer for 5 minutes. Strain, keeping the stock.

Melt the butter in a pan, add the onion, carrots and parsley and cook gently until soft, about 5 minutes. Mix in the flour and cook for a further 2 minutes. Gradually add the stock and the wine and cook gently until the mixture has thickened. Remove from the heat.

Beat the egg yolks with the cream and pour into the mixture in the pan. Add the prawns, return the pan to gentle heat and cook, stirring continuously, until slightly thickened. Do not allow to boil. Season to taste and serve at once.

Amêijoas à Bulhão Pato
(Clams à Bulhão Pato)

Bulhão Pato was a nineteenth-century poet now remembered for this recipe rather than for his poetry.

Mussels can be used successfully for this recipe and are more easily obtainable than clams.

Serves four

3 lb. clams or mussels	2 fl. oz. olive oil
½ pint water	1 handful coriander, chopped
3 cloves garlic, crushed	seasoning

Wash the clams or mussels very thoroughly in several waters, scraping off any barnacles from the shells and removing the beards. Discard any which remain open, as this shows they are dead.

In a large saucepan bring the water, garlic, oil and coriander to the boil. Put in the clams or mussels, cover and boil until they have opened, about 5 minutes. Cook for a further minute. Taste and season if necessary.

Sopa de congro
(Conger Eel Soup)

This is a very thick and substantial soup. In Portugal fresh prawns would be used to make it. As they are difficult to obtain in this country, I have substituted cooked prawns, but used the shells, heads and tails to flavour the stock.

Serves four

2 oz. prawns (in shells)
1 lb. conger eel
1 pint water
1 carrot, sliced
1 sprig parsley, chopped
1 pinch paprika
1 bay leaf

salt
3 medium sized onions, sliced
1 medium sized potato, sliced
2 tomatoes, chopped
1 tablespoon olive oil
1 oz. butter
1½ oz. grated Parmesan cheese

Wash and shell the prawns, keeping separately the flesh and the shells, heads and tails.

Cut the eel into 5 or 6 pieces and put into a large saucepan with the water, carrot, parsley, paprika, bay leaf, salt and one of the onions. Cover and simmer over gentle heat until the eel is cooked, about 15 minutes. Strain, return the liquid to the pan, and, after discarding the bay leaf, keep the other ingredients warm.

Add the prawn shells, heads and tails to the liquid in the pan, cover and cook gently for 5 minutes. Strain, return the stock to the pan and add the potato and tomatoes. Cover and cook until the potato is tender. Skin, bone and flake the eel and sieve, or liquidize, along with the other ingredients cooked with it and the contents of the pan.

Heat the oil and butter in a frying pan and cook the remaining 2 onions until limp and golden. Return the sieved mixture to the saucepan, add the onions, prawns and cheese and heat through gently, stirring all the time.

Canja de galinha à Alentejana
(Alentejan Chicken Soup)

Serves four

1½ pints chicken stock
3 oz. *linguiça* (see p. 18) *or*
 garlic sausage, chopped
4 oz. rice, cooked

a good squeeze of lemon juice
seasoning
2 handfuls fresh mint,
 chopped

Heat the stock and add the *linguiça*, rice and lemon juice. Season to taste and serve sprinkled with the chopped mint.

Sopa de Entrudo
(Shrove-tide Soup, from Elvas)

Serves four

2 oz. small cubes bread
1½ pints chicken stock
4 egg yolks

juice of half a lemon
seasoning

Toast the bread cubes in a medium oven.

Heat the stock. Beat the egg yolks, add the lemon juice and gradually mix in 4 tablespoons of the stock.

Place the bread cubes in a soup tureen, add the egg mixture and pour over the rest of the hot stock. Season and serve.

Fish

The fish of Portugal is plentiful, varied and delicious. This is not surprising considering that the country has an extensive coastline and that no place is further than 140 miles from the sea. Even the towns lying near the Spanish border always have supplies of fresh fish in their markets.

Bacalhau, which is dried, salted cod, is a subject so dear to the heart of the Portuguese that I have already given it pride of place in my section on ingredients.

Many districts have their own fish speciality. In the Minho, in the north of Portugal, the lamprey is considered a great delicacy; and it is not unusual for the lover of good food from Oporto, that city of gourmets, to travel some distance north to the region round the Minho river, near the Spanish border, where the lampreys are caught, and indulge in a large and tasty meal of *lampreia à moda do Minho*. Because it is difficult, if not impossible, to buy lampreys in this country, and because the preparation and cooking in the Portuguese manner is complicated, I have not included a recipe.

However, if you visit the north of Portugal, try to have a dish of *lampreia à moda do Minho*.

Farther south along the coast lies Nazaré. Once a small fishing town, it has become one of the best-known tourist places on the Atlantic coast. This has sadly spoilt it, and it is not unusual for visitors to be pestered by touts and beggars, though it is the only place in Portugal where I have ever had this experience. The locals often stand ready to pose for a photograph, expecting to be paid afterwards. Yet otherwise it is an attractive place, with its large curved bay backed by high cliffs, and the local costume is colourful and individual. The men wear brightly-coloured checked shirts and black woollen caps with long tassels, and the women innumerable petticoats: I believe sixteen is not unusual. Both the distinctive features of the people and the shape of the high-prowed boats are said to be Phoenician in origin. Oxen, which live on the beach, are used to haul the boats up on to the sands.

Nazaré also has a large and noisy fish auction, but one which I think has more character is that at Sesimbra. Here the auction is held each morning and evening on the beach, and it is quite an experience to see the *espadarte* or swordfish laid out on the sand, large and glistening, and to listen to the animated bidding.

Lulas and *polvo* – squid and octopus – are to be found in most Portuguese fish markets, though possibly rather more in the south, and both appear frequently on Portuguese menus. There are a number of ways of cooking them and, if cooked carefully and not allowed to toughen, they are delicious.

The beaches of the Algarve, now so well known, are still attractive and virtually unspoilt; and the boats, many with a symbol painted on their bows, such as the eye which is thought to ward off evil, make a colourful scene on the fishing beaches. On the sands above the boats the nets are spread out and are mended by the older men. The catches here are mainly of tunny and sardines, the latter being canned and sent all over the world. One thing, however, which has always puzzled me is that I have never seen in Portugal the small sardines we get in tins. I think this size must be reserved for canning only.

Finally a word about the *varinas* of Lisbon. These are the fish porter women and are unique to Lisbon and worth looking out for during a visit to that city. They are usually of magnificent physique, more like men than women, and this is emphasized by the fact that many of them have quite a moustache. They walk erect and barefooted and I believe that like their counterparts in the north, the fisherwomen of Leith in Scotland, they have strident voices, though I have never heard them myself.

Filetes de linguado à Portuguesa
(Fillets of Sole)

Serves four

2 soles, 1 lb. each, whole	6 fl. oz. water
seasoning	3 oz. butter
4 fl. oz. dry white wine	¾ lb. ripe tomatoes, skinned
2 medium sized onions, sliced	and chopped
1 carrot, sliced	1 sprig parsley, chopped
1 bay leaf	

Fillet the fish, keeping the heads and bones. Place the fillets in an oven-proof dish, season and pour over half the wine. Put the heads and bones in a saucepan together with one onion, the carrot, the bay leaf, the water and the remaining wine. Season, cover and cook over gentle heat for about an hour. Strain and reserve the stock.

Melt 1 oz. of the butter in a saucepan, add the tomatoes, the other onion and the parsley and cook over gentle heat until the liquid has almost evaporated, about 15 minutes.

Meanwhile, pour over the fish 4 tablespoonfuls of the reserved stock, dot with 1 oz. of the butter and cook in a moderate oven (350° F., gas 4) until it loses its translucency (about 8 minutes).

Put the rest of the stock in a saucepan and reduce over moderate heat to about 3 fl. oz. When the tomato mixture is cooked add this to it, with the last ounce of the butter, and season to taste.

When the fish is cooked, place it on a serving dish and surround it with the tomato mixture.

Linguados inteiros com recheio de camarão à Lisboeta

(Sole with Prawn Stuffing, from Lisbon)

Serves four

¾ lb. prawns in shells
3 fl. oz. water
2½ oz. butter
1 oz. flour
3 fl. oz. milk
1 teaspoon tabasco sauce
seasoning

4 medium soles, unfilleted
a purée made from 3
 medium-sized potatoes
1 tablespoon breadcrumbs
1 tablespoon grated Parmesan
 cheese

Shell the prawns, keeping separately the flesh and the shells, heads and tails. Place the latter in a small saucepan with the water, cover, and simmer gently for 5 minutes. Strain and reserve the stock.

Melt 1½ oz. of the butter in a saucepan, mix in the flour and cook gently for 2 minutes. Gradually add the prawn stock and the milk, stirring continuously, and when the sauce has thickened add the prawns and tabasco sauce and season to taste.

Remove the black skin from the soles (the fishmonger will usually do this for you). Make a slit from head to tail, carefully raise the flesh from the bone and stuff with the prawn mixture. Place the fish side by side in a buttered oven-proof dish, sprinkle with a little salt, dot with ½ oz. of the butter and bake in a hot oven (440° F., gas 7) until cooked, about 20 minutes.

With the potato purée make a border round the edge of an oven-proof serving dish, place the fish in the middle, dot with the remaining butter and sprinkle with the breadcrumbs and the Parmesan cheese. Put in a moderate oven until heated through and lightly browned.

Pudim de peixe com macarrão à Lisboeta
(Macaroni and Fish Pudding, Lisbon Style)

Serves four

½ lb. macaroni	½ lb. white fish fillets, skinned
2 oz. butter	and cut into small pieces
1½ oz. flour	seasoning
12 fl. oz. milk	1 tablespoon fine breadcrumbs
2 eggs, beaten	

Boil the macaroni in a large saucepan containing 3 pints of boiling salted water for 10 minutes. Remove from the heat, drain and keep warm.

Melt the butter in a saucepan, stir in the flour and cook gently for 2 minutes. Gradually add the milk, stirring continuously, and cook until thickened. Remove from the heat, add the beaten eggs, the macaroni and the fish, and season to taste.

Butter an 8-inch oven-proof mould, sprinkle with the breadcrumbs and pour in the fish mixture. Bake in a hot oven (440° F., gas 7) until the fish is cooked, about ½ hour. Turn out on to a dish and serve with a *tomatada à Portuguesa* (see p. 89).

Escabeche de savel
(Fish Vinaigrette)

An *escabeche* is a pickle for fish. It is used a great deal in Portuguese cooking and for a number of different kinds of fish. The particular *escabeche* I have given is for *savel*, shad, which is a common fish in Portugal. However, any firm, white fish fillets can be used.

Serves four

about 7 fl. oz. cooking oil	6 peppercorns
1½ lb. white fish fillets	1 teaspoon paprika
2 onions, sliced	2 teaspoons salt
4 fl. oz. olive oil	1 bay leaf
6 cloves garlic, crushed	2 tablespoons dry white wine
2 carrots, grated	4 fl. oz. white wine vinegar
1 small bunch parsley, chopped	

Heat the cooking oil in a large frying pan and fry the fish until it is cooked and flakes easily. Allow to cool slightly and then remove the skin and flake into pieces. Put into a dish with a cover.

Prepare the *escabeche* as follows. In a frying pan, cook the onions gently in the olive oil until they are golden. Remove from the heat and stir in the garlic, grated carrots, parsley, peppercorns, paprika, salt, bay leaf, wine and vinegar. Cool and pour over the fish.

Cover the dish and chill for at least 24 hours. Serve with baked potatoes.

Pescada escondida
(Disguised Whiting)

Pescada is whiting and in this dish is served cold, which is unusual and very good.

Serves four

1½ lb. whiting fillet	salt to taste
1 onion, sliced	5 large potatoes, cooked and
1 sprig parsley, chopped	finely mashed
1 tablespoon olive oil	grated black pepper
1 tablespoon wine vinegar	2 hard-boiled eggs, chopped
6 peppercorns	parsley for garnish
3 cloves garlic, crushed	2 oz. black olives

Put the fish in a pan with the onion, parsley, oil, vinegar, peppercorns, garlic and salt and just enough water to cover. Simmer until cooked, about 15 minutes. Remove the fish and strain and keep the stock.

Skin and flake the fish and put it into a dish. Cover with the mashed potatoes and sprinkle with a little of the stock; but do not make too moist. Season with a little black pepper and garnish with the eggs, parsley and olives. Serve cold.

Pescada à Viriato
(Whiting in the mode of the Viriato)

This is one of several recipes I was given at the Estalagem Viriato, a small hotel at Vila Meã, 8 km. east of Viseu, in the region of Beira Alta. Beautifully situated among woods and overlooking a deep mountain gorge, this *estalagem* we consider one of the best in Portugal. Viriato was a shepherd who lived and tended his sheep in the surrounding hills and became famous for his resistance to the Roman invasion.

Serves four

1 lb. potatoes	seasoned flour
olive oil	chopped parsley
cooking oil for frying	lettuce
1½ lb. fillets of whiting or	1 onion, sliced
other white fish, cut into	3 oz. black olives
convenient pieces	

Scrub the potatoes but do not peel. Boil them in salted water until tender. Skin and cut into dice. Mix with some olive oil while still warm.

Heat some cooking oil in a frying pan. Lightly cover the fish with the seasoned flour and fry it until it is cooked and golden brown on both sides.

Serve the fish with the potatoes, garnished with chopped parsley, and a salad made with the lettuce, sliced onion and black olives and tossed in olive oil.

Caldeirada de peixe – Algarve
(Fish Stew from the Algarve)

Most regions of Portugal have their own way of making *caldeirada* and many different kinds of fish go into the making, from white fish and sardines to lobsters and mussels.

The recipe I was given used fresh sardines the Portuguese sardines which are much larger than those we find in our tins. I have used large sprats.

This then is the way they make *caldeirada* in the Algarve, hot and spicy with a strong flavour of garlic.

Four good servings

½ lb. large sprats	½ teaspoon grated nutmeg
½ lb. haddock fillet	1 dessertspoon *piri-piri* (see
½ lb. plaice fillet	p. 18) *or* tabasco sauce
½ lb. eel	3 peppercorns
salt	1 green pepper, sliced
2 fl. oz. olive oil	2 fl. oz. dry white wine
3 onions, sliced	1 tablespoon white wine
6 cloves garlic, crushed	vinegar
1 lb. tomatoes, chopped	½ oz. butter
1 handful parsley, chopped	4 thick slices bread, crust
1 bay leaf	removed

Remove the heads from the sprats and cut the other fish into smallish pieces. Lightly cover with salt and leave for 1 hour.

Heat the oil in a heavy casserole, add the onions and cook until soft. Add the garlic, tomatoes, parsley and bay leaf. Season with salt, nutmeg, *piri-piri* and peppercorns and simmer gently until the tomatoes are cooked. Remove from the casserole and keep warm.

Wash the salt off the fish and pat dry. Put layers of the different fish in the casserole, with the fish that takes longest to cook at the bottom and the sprats at the top. Between the layers place the sliced pepper and the tomato–onion mixture. Add the wine and vinegar. Melt the butter and pour it over, then place the bread slices on top. Cover the casserole and cook in a moderate oven (350° F., gas 4) for 20 minutes. The sauce should cover the bread slices during the cooking.

Caldeirada à Ribatejana

(Ribatejo Fish Stew)

Serves four

2 fl. oz. olive oil	1 large clove garlic, crushed
1 medium-sized onion, sliced	½ pint water
1 lb. mullet	seasoning
1 lb. eel	¾ lb. potatoes, sliced
2 large tomatoes, chopped	

Heat the oil in a large saucepan and cook the onion gently until limp and golden. Skin and bone the fish, cut it into pieces and add it together with the tomatoes, garlic, water and seasoning. Cover and simmer over gentle heat for 10 minutes. Then add the potatoes and continue to simmer until both fish and potatoes are cooked, about 10 minutes.

Trutas à moda de Bragança
(Bragança Trout)

Serves four

¼ lb. lean *presunto* (see p. 18) *or* ham, chopped	4 trout
olive oil	seasoned flour
	1 lemon, cut into quarters

Cook the *presunto* gently for a few minutes in a little olive oil in a frying pan. Remove and keep warm. Heat some more olive oil in the pan. Roll the fish in the seasoned flour and cook them quickly in the oil, turning once. Serve with the chopped *presunto* sprinkled over and garnished with lemon quarters.

Salmonetes grelhados à Setúbalense
(Grilled Red Mullet from Setúbal)

Serves four

4 red mullet	4 tablespoons water
cooking oil	1 sprig parsley, chopped
seasoning	a good squeeze of lemon
¼ lb. butter	juice
1 oz. flour	1 lemon for garnishing

Clean the fish, reserving the livers. Brush with oil, season and grill under a gentle heat until cooked, turning once.

Mash the livers. Melt the butter in a pan, mix in the flour and cook for a few minutes. Add the water and make a sauce. Put in the livers, parsley, lemon juice and seasoning and cook gently for a further few minutes, until the livers are cooked.

Serve the fish with the sauce poured over and garnished with lemon quarters.

Sardinhas assadas

(Grilled Sardines)

In Portugal sardines cooked this way are usually done over a
fogareiro, a small cast-iron brazier with a raised grate on which
charcoal is burned; the sardines are cooked on a grid over the
coals. It is a perfect way to cook the large, succulent sardines
caught in the waters off Portugal, and the smell of the fish cooking,
frequently in the open air, is one of my memories of Portuguese
cooking.

The sardines must be fresh, not tinned. If you cannot get fresh
sardines, large sprats can be used, but the flavour will not be quite
the same.

It is difficult to buy a *fogareiro* in this country, and with our
weather it is seldom possible to cook outside, so I have suggested
simply that the sardines should be grilled.

Serves four

12 medium-sized sardines	4 bay leaves
coarse salt	1 onion, sliced in rings
2 large green peppers, sliced	2 oz. black olives
olive oil	vinegar

Wash the sardines and remove any scales. Sprinkle with coarse
salt and leave for about 1 hour. Wash them again under running
water to remove any excess salt.

Put the green peppers in an ovenproof dish, season and sprinkle
with olive oil. Cook in a moderate oven (350° F., gas 4) until limp
and slightly charred, about 20 minutes.

Brush the grill pan and the sardines with a little olive oil, and
put them, with the bay leaves on top, under a hot grill. Cook for
about 10 minutes, removing the bay leaves and turning once after a
few minutes. Reduce the heat towards the end of the cooking.

Serve the fish with the peppers, raw onion rings and black olives,
and with boiled potatoes. Sprinkle the fish with vinegar.

Bacalhau à Gomes de Sá

Serves four

1½ lb. dried salt cod
½ pint olive oil
2 onions, sliced
1 lb. cooked potatoes, sliced

2 oz. black olives
1 clove garlic, crushed
4 hard-boiled eggs
chopped parsley

Soak the cod in cold water for 24 hours, changing the water several times, then simmer until tender in just enough water to cover (2–3 hours). Remove the skin and bones and flake into large pieces. Heat the oil in a heavy casserole, put in the onions and cook gently until soft. Add the potatoes, cod, olives and garlic and bake in a moderate oven (350° F., gas 4) until browned, about 10 minutes. Garnish with quartered eggs and sprinkle with the parsley.

Bacalhau à brás

Serves four

1½ lb. dried salt cod
4 fl. oz. olive oil
2 large onions, sliced

1 lb. cooked potatoes
2 oz. black olives
8 eggs

Soak the cod for 24 hours in cold water, changing the water several times, then simmer, in just enough water to cover, until tender (2–3 hours). Remove the skin and bones and flake into large pieces. Heat the oil in a large frying pan and sauté the onions until golden. Slice the potatoes. Add them, the fish and the olives to the onions and cook for 10 minutes, turning frequently. Beat the eggs and add them to the fish mixture. Simmer until the eggs are cooked.

Bacalhau à moda de Minho

(Cod in the Minho Style)

Serves four

4 thick steaks of dried salt cod
cabbage leaves

3 tablespoons olive oil
1 lb. onions, sliced

Soak the dried cod in cold water for at least 24 hours, to remove the salt, changing the water once or twice. Wrap up each cod steak in a cabbage leaf and tie with thin string. Put in an ovenproof dish and cook in a moderate oven (350° F., gas 4) for about 40 minutes or until the fish is tender and the cabbage leaves have turned brownish like tobacco leaves. Carefully remove the string and pieces of cabbage. Place the cod on a serving dish and keep warm.

Heat the oil in a frying pan. Add the onions and cook gently until soft. Cover the fish with the onions and serve.

The dish should be accompanied by potatoes boiled in their skins and peeled when cooked.

Bacalhau com pimentos e tomates à Alentejana

(Salted Cod with Peppers and Tomatoes in the Mode of the Alentejo)

Serves four

1½ lb. salted cod	5 tomatoes, sliced
1 lb. potatoes	seasoning
5 tablespoons olive oil	black olives for garnish
4 green peppers, seeded and sliced	

Soak the cod in cold water for 24 hours, changing the water several times. Put it in a pan with just enough water to cover and simmer until tender, about 2–3 hours.

Boil the unpeeled potatoes in salted water until tender.

Heat one tablespoon olive oil in a casserole, add the sliced peppers, and cook until just limp, about 10 minutes. Take them out and put in layers of the sliced potatoes, the fish and the tomatoes and peppers. Season and sprinkle with the rest of the oil. Bake in a moderate oven (350° F., gas 4) for about ½ hour until the mixture is heated through and lightly browned.

Serve in the casserole, with a garnish of black olives.

Lulas fritas com mayonnaise
(Fried Squid with Mayonnaise)

Serves four

1½ lb. squid
oil for frying
1 tinned pimento, cut into
   strips, for garnish

For the Mayonnaise
1 egg yolk
½ teaspoon dry mustard
1 teaspoon white vinegar
seasoning
¼ pint olive oil

Make a mayonnaise in the usual way.

Pull the heads of the squid from the bodies, remove and discard the spines and internal organs, cut off the tentacles just below the eyes and discard the heads. Thoroughly wash the bodies, wing flesh and tentacles, cut into smallish pieces and season.

Heat the oil in a frying pan and fry the squid pieces over a moderate heat until cooked, about 8–10 minutes. Do not over-cook, as they will become tough.

Garnish with the pimento and mayonnaise and serve with boiled potatoes.

Lulas de caldeirada
(Squid Stew)

Serves four

2 lb. squid
2 fl. oz. olive oil
2 large onions, sliced
1 teaspoon curry powder
½ teaspoon powdered ginger
½ lb. tomatoes, chopped

1 bay leaf
salt to taste
1 glass dry white wine
4 medium potatoes, peeled
   and sliced
2 pimentoes, sliced

Pull the heads of the squid from the bodies, remove and discard the spines and internal organs, cut off the tentacles just below the eyes and discard the heads. Thoroughly wash the bodies, wing flesh and tentacles, and cut into smallish pieces.

Heat the oil in a heavy casserole, put in the onions and cook gently until soft. Add the curry powder, ginger, squid, tomatoes, bay leaf, salt and wine, cover and cook gently for 1½ hours.

Finally add the potatoes and pimentoes, and a very little water if necessary to cook them, and cook gently until the potatoes are tender, about 25 minutes.

Lulas recheadas
(Stuffed Squid)

Serves four

4 medium sized squid about ½ lb. each	1 sprig tarragon, chopped
3 fl. oz. olive oil	seasoning
2 onions, sliced	2 egg yolks
2 hard-boiled eggs, chopped	2 oz. butter
3 oz. ham, chopped	2 tablespoons tomato purée
1 large sprig parsley, chopped	6 oz. Patna rice

Pull the heads of the squid from the bodies and remove and discard the spines and internal organs. Wash very well. Cut off and chop the wing flesh and tentacles, discarding the heads.

Heat the oil and put in the onions. Cook gently and when golden and limp add the hard-boiled eggs, the ham, the tentacles and wing flesh, the parsley, tarragon and seasoning. Bind the mixture with the beaten egg yolks and with it stuff the squid bodies, closing the openings with cocktail sticks.

Melt 1 oz. butter in a casserole and add the tomato purée and enough water to make a thin sauce. Put in the squid, cover and cook in a moderate oven (350° F., gas 4) until the squid are tender, about ¾ hour.

Cook the rice in boiling salted water until tender (about 12 minutes) and drain. Melt the rest of the butter and to it add the rice. Mix well.

Make a circle of rice, put the squid in the centre and pour the sauce over. Serve at once.

Eirós grelhada à moda do Ribatejo
(Grilled Eel in the Ribatejo Manner)

Serves four

1½ lb. eel	1 tablespoon lemon juice
2 oz. butter	seasoning
1 large handful parsley, chopped	

Wash the eel very thoroughly and cut into 2-inch pieces. Melt the butter and add the parsley, lemon juice and seasoning. Dip the eel pieces in the butter mixture and place them under a hot grill. Keep the butter mixture warm. Grill the eel until cooked, about 10–15 minutes, turning to brown lightly on all sides, and reducing the heat towards the end of cooking. Serve with the butter mixture poured over.

Enguias à Aveirense
(Aveiro Cold Grilled Eels)

We had been looking for a good restaurant in Lisbon that did not cater for tourists. We were recommended to go to one near the river, in the dock area. We had some difficulty in finding it and got lost several times in narrow cobbled streets festooned with washing. When we did find the restaurant, we were not impressed. Its furnishing was bare in the extreme and its clientele appeared to be local habituées. They eyed us rather curiously, but as the meal progressed they seemed to decide we were all right and acceptable.

The first course we ordered was *enguias à Aveirense*. This was cold, grilled eels in a marinade. They were served tail to mouth, in the way that whiting used to be served. The flavour was curious, but in spite of the many bones, we decided it was really good.

Serves four

1½ lb. small eels	1 bay leaf
oil for grilling	1 clove garlic, crushed
4 fl. oz. dry white wine	salt
4 fl. oz. white wine vinegar	black pepper
1 sprig parsley, chopped	

Clean the eels. Fix the tails inside the mouths to form a circle, and season. Brush with the oil, place under a hot grill and cook for about 10 minutes, turning from time to time and reducing the heat towards the end. Place in a dish and allow to cool.

Make a marinade with the wine, vinegar, parsley, bay leaf, garlic and seasoning. Pour it over the eels. Cover and chill for 24 hours before serving.

Congro ensopado à moda de Bragança
(Conger Eel Stew from Bragança)

This recipe comes from Bragança, the capital of the Trás-os-Montes region. Bragança lies in the mountains in the north-east corner of the country, well inland, but however far one is from the sea in Portugal it is almost always possible to buy fresh fish, as this recipe indicates.

Serves four

3 tablespoons olive oil	seasoning
1 medium onion, sliced	4 thick slices bread, crusts
1½ lb. conger eel, in 4 slices	removed
1 teaspoon wine vinegar	3 egg yolks
4 fl. oz. water	1 sprig parsley, chopped
1 bay leaf	

Heat the oil in a heavy casserole, add the onion and cook over gentle heat until limp and golden. Place the slices of fish on top of the onion, add the vinegar, water, bay leaf and seasoning, cover and cook in a moderate oven (350° F., gas 4) until the fish loses its translucency, about 20 minutes. Do not overcook or it will become tough.

Remove from the oven, lift out the fish and onion on to a plate, discard the bay leaf and pour off and reserve the sauce. Put the slices of bread in the bottom of the casserole, place the slices of fish on top and keep warm.

Beat the egg yolks with the parsley and, while continuing to beat, gradually add the warm sauce. Pour into a small pan and cook over gentle heat, stirring continuously, until the mixture thickens slightly. Do not allow to boil.

Pour the sauce over the fish and serve very hot accompanied by *grão com tomatada* (see p. 86).

Lagosta à moda de Peniche
(Lobster in Peniche Style)

The recipe I was given for this dish uses a live lobster, but I use a lobster which has already been killed and cooked.

The recipe comes from Peniche, on the western coast of Portugal, and the nearby Berlenga islands, where it is a great speciality, many small restaurants having their own particular ingredients.

Serves four

4 fl. oz. olive oil	½ teaspoon paprika
1 large onion, sliced	1 wineglass dry white wine
4 tomatoes, sliced	½ wineglass brandy
1 sprig parsley, chopped	salt
1 sprig thyme, chopped	ground black pepper
2 cloves garlic, crushed	1½ oz. butter
1 bay leaf	2 lobsters about 1 lb. each,
2 red chillies	cooked
¼ teaspoon grated nutmeg	1 wineglass port

Heat the oil in a saucepan, add the onion, tomatoes, parsley, thyme, garlic, bay leaf, chillies, nutmeg, paprika, white wine and brandy, and season to taste with salt and black pepper. Cover and cook gently until the mixture has considerably thickened, about 20–30 minutes.

Melt the butter in a casserole and put in the lobster meat and the mixture in alternate layers. Pour over the port, cover and put in a slow oven (280° F., gas 1) until thoroughly heated, about 20 minutes.

Amêijoas à Portuguesa
(Portuguese Clams or Mussels)

Amêijoas are clams, but as it is not always easy to buy clams in this country I have given mussels as an alternative.

Serves four

4 lb. clams or mussels	4 cloves garlic, crushed
5 tablespoons olive oil	1 sprig parsley
1 bay leaf	seasoning

Wash the clams or mussels very thoroughly, removing the beards and any barnacles. Discard any which are open and will not close when tapped, as this indicates that they are dead.

Heat the oil in a large pan and add the bay leaf, garlic, parsley and seasoning. When the garlic is slightly browned add the clams or mussels. Cover and cook over gentle heat until they have all opened, about 5–10 minutes. Serve very hot.

Amêijoas na cataplana
(Clams or Mussels in a Cataplana)

A *cataplana* is a large frying pan with a tightly fitting lid. It is used for quite a number of Portuguese recipes, particularly those of the Algarve. I do not think it is possible to buy a *cataplana* in this country, but a heavy casserole with a tightly fitting lid will do equally well.

This recipe is for clams cooked in their shells with chopped sausage and ham. As in other recipes for *amêijoas*, I have given mussels as an alternative, these being more easily obtainable in this country. The combination of shell fish and meats is unusual and very good.

Serves four

2 lb. clams or mussels
1 oz. butter
1 tablespoon olive oil
3 onions, sliced
½ teaspoon paprika
1 tablespoon *piri-piri* (see (p. 18)

3 oz. *presunto* (see p. 18) *or* ham, chopped
3 oz. *chouriço* (see p. 18) *or* garlic sausage, chopped
1 clove garlic, crushed
1 handful parsley, chopped

Wash the clams or mussels thoroughly, scraping off any barnacles and removing the beards. Discard any which are open and will not close when tapped, as this indicates that they are dead.

Heat the butter and oil in a heavy casserole over moderate heat, add the onions and the seasonings, and cook until the onions are soft. Add the clams or mussels, meats, garlic and parsley. Cover the casserole and cook over moderate heat for 20 minutes.

Serve immediately, uncovering the casserole at the table.

Camarões com vinho do porto
(Prawns with Port Wine)

Serves four

½ lb. shelled prawns	8 egg yolks
2 oz. butter	2 tablespoons double cream
2 medium onions, sliced	seasoning
2 tablespoons dry port	

Cut the prawns into small pieces. Melt the butter in a frying pan. Add the onions and cook over a medium heat until soft and golden. Add the prawns and cook gently for about 5 minutes. Pour over the port and simmer for a few more minutes. Beat the egg yolks with the cream and seasoning. Take the frying pan off the heat and mix the eggs and cream into the prawn mixture. Pour into ramekins and cook in a moderate oven until the eggs have just set.

Arroz de camarões
(Rice with Prawns)

Serves four

2 tablespoons oil or butter	parsley and thyme, finely
2 onions, chopped	chopped
2 pimentoes, sliced	1 bay leaf
½ oz. flour	salt
milk	¼ lb. shelled prawns
5 tomatoes, peeled and	
chopped	

Melt the butter or heat the oil and sauté the onions and pimentoes until soft. Add the flour. Cook for a few minutes, then gradually add enough milk to make a fairly thick white sauce. Add the tomatoes, herbs, bay leaf and salt to taste. Cook slowly for a further 30 minutes, adding the prawns for the last ten minutes. Remove the bay leaf and serve with rice.

Arroz de salmão à Lisboeta

(Rice with Salmon, Lisbon Style)

This is a recipe for fresh salmon, but it can also be made with tinned salmon or tuna. The tinned fish, being already cooked, need only be flaked and added to the sauce and heated through.

Serves four

arroz de manteiga (see p. 92)	2 oz. flour
1 teaspoon curry powder	¾ pint milk
¾ lb. fresh salmon, in 3 slices	2 egg yolks, beaten
oil	seasoning
3 oz. butter	

Make the *arroz de manteiga*, adding the curry powder with the stock. Keep hot.

Lightly brush the grid of a grill pan and the fish slices with a little oil and grill the fish under moderate heat until tender, turning once. Take from the heat and when cool enough remove and discard the skin and bones and flake the flesh. Keep warm.

Melt the butter in a saucepan, mix in the flour and cook gently for 2 minutes. Then gradually add the milk and cook until thickened. Finally add the beaten egg yolks and cook gently, stirring continuously, until they are cooked. Do not allow to boil. Season to taste. Add the fish and mix well.

To serve, put the rice in the centre of a serving dish and pour over the fish mixture.

Atum com arroz

(Tunny with Rice)

In Portugal fresh tunny is always used for this dish, but tinned tuna will do just as well.

Serves four

½ lb. cooked fresh tunny *or* 1 large tin tuna	2 large, firm tomatoes, chopped
8 oz. cold, cooked Patna rice	2 oz. black olives, stoned and chopped
4 fl. oz. mayonnaise	seasoning
a small quantity of crisp lettuce, shredded	2 hard-boiled eggs

Flake the fish and put it into a bowl together with the rice, mayonnaise, lettuce, tomatoes and olives. Add seasoning to taste. Put the mixture into a mould, press well down and chill. Turn out and serve garnished with slices of egg.

Atum ao molho verde
(Tunny Salad)

The region round Castelo de Vide in the Alentejo is so far little known to holiday visitors. It is away from the coast and not far from the Serra da Estrela, the high and wild range of mountains separating Portugal and Spain. Wolves and wild boar still live in the remoter parts and have been known to come down to the villages in the depth of winter.

Castelo de Vide is a good centre from which to explore this area and there is at least one good *estalagem*. The town is surrounded by wooded slopes, and as we sat on our balcony after a good dinner the sound of the cicadas and frogs was almost deafening. It was in the Estalagem de São Paulo where we stayed that we had this tunny salad.

Fresh tunny would be used for this dish in Portugal, but tinned tuna will do equally well.

Serves four

1 crisp cabbage lettuce	3 tomatoes, sliced
2 medium onions	3 tablespoons olive oil
1 lb. cooked fresh tunny *or* two 7-oz. tins tuna	

Reserve several of the larger lettuce leaves for garnish. Finely shred the rest and slice the onions. If tinned tuna is used, drain the oil. Flake the fish and put it in a bowl with the shredded lettuce, the onions and the tomatoes. Add the olive oil and mix well. Serve the mixture on the large lettuce leaves.

Salada de atum Albufeirense
(Tunny Salad Albufeirense)

Serves four

½ lb. cooked fresh tunny *or*
  1 large tin tuna
mayonnaise to mix, roughly
  ¼ pint
4 hard-boiled eggs, chopped

1 lb. cooked sliced french
  beans
3 oz. black olives
tomatoes and cucumber for
  garnish

If tinned tuna is used, drain off the oil.

Flake the fish and add the mayonnaise, eggs and beans. Serve garnished with black olives, tomato quarters and sliced cucumber.

Meat

Though I personally have not found it so, it is said that in Portugal the meat, or more particularly the beef, is often tough. Nevertheless there are some very good meat dishes, notably *cozido*, a stew of many different kinds of meat including beef, chicken and sausage, the flavouring differing from district to district.

Liver is eaten throughout Portugal. It is particularly prized in Lisbon, where it is marinated overnight in wine, vinegar and spices with plenty of garlic and then fried. This is quite the nicest way, I think, of cooking liver, and it never seems to be tough or dry.

Quite a few people have an aversion to tripe. As a child often fed rather frugally on a Scots menu of herrings and tripe, I enjoy it; and even those who feel an aversion should enjoy both *dobrada* and *tripas à moda do Porto*, in which a number of other kinds of meat and flavourings are added.

Whatever may be said about Portuguese beef, the pork is certainly not tough, and some of the most delicious dishes are made with this meat. Except in the Ribatejo region, the land is not generally suitable for grazing, and consequently the amount of cattle reared is small; but large herds of pigs are raised in the wilder regions of the north and in the Alentejo, where they roam under the trees and live on a diet of truffles and acorns.

The Bairrada region near Coimbra is well known for its dishes of *leitão* or sucking pig. Though it is not always easy to buy a sucking pig in this country, I have included a recipe.

Sausages and hams are specialities of the country, probably rather more in the northern regions, where the hams of Chaves and Lamego are famous. The flavouring of the sausages differs from region to region and they are used considerably in cooking.

Chickens appear quite frequently on Portuguese menus, and are cooked in many ways. One which is unusual and worth trying is *frangos no espeto à Minha moda*, in which the chicken is brushed with olive oil and *piri-piri* (hot chilli sauce) and roasted on a spit.

Finally a word about game in Portugal. This is varied and plentiful, especially in the regions near the Spanish border, which are a paradise for the sportsman. There are many recipes for game, particularly for partridges and rabbits.

Cozido à Beira Alta
(Meat Stew from Beira Alta)

A *cozido* is a meat stew and all manner of things seem to go into it, such as shanks of veal and beef, ox tails, pig's trotters, sausages and whole chickens.

The kinds of meat vary according to region; this recipe comes from Guarda, in the Beira Alta. One of the specialities here is *morcela* sausage, a blood sausage spiced with cumin. I do not think it is possible to buy *morcela* in this country, but black puddings can be used, with the addition of ground cumin, and the flavour will be very much the same.

Four large servings

4 pints water	½ lb. cabbage, thickly sliced
1 lb. beef, cut into cubes	½ lb. turnips, peeled and thickly
1 ham or bacon bone	sliced

1 teaspoon ground cumin
salt and pepper
2 chicken pieces, weighing
    together about about ¾ lb.
½ lb. black pudding, thickly
    sliced

1 stick celery, cut into pieces
2 potatoes, peeled and thickly
    sliced
1 oz. butter
1 onion, sliced
¼ lb. Patna rice

Bring the water to the boil in a large pan, add the beef, the bone, the cumin and seasoning and simmer gently for 3 hours, removing any scum. Then add the chicken and simmer for a further 30 minutes.

Remove a pint of the stock and set it aside, then put in the black pudding and the vegetables, except the onion, and cook for a further 30 minutes.

Meanwhile melt the butter in another saucepan, put in the onion and cook gently until soft. Add the rice and cook for a few minutes and finally pour in the pint of stock. Cover the pan and cook over gentle heat until the rice is tender and all the moisture has been absorbed, about 30 minutes.

Remove the chicken meat from the bones, place all the meat and vegetables on a large serving dish and serve with the rice.

The stock will make an excellent soup.

Bifes de cebolada

(Steak with Onion Sauce)

Serves four

3 tablespoons olive oil
2 large onions, sliced
1 tablespoon white vinegar
2 tablespoons tomato purée
2 cloves garlic, crushed

1 sprig parsley, chopped
seasoning
4 pieces rump steak about
    1½ lb. in all
oil for grilling

To make the *cebolada* heat the 3 tablespoons of olive oil in a *frigideira* or large frying pan, put in the onion slices and cook gently until soft. Mix the vinegar with the tomato purée and add to the onions together with the garlic, parsley and seasoning. Cover the pan and simmer until the mixture is blended and softened, about 10 minutes.

Brush the steak with oil and grill according to taste. Cover with the *cebolada* and serve.

Bife grelhado à Viriato
(Grilled Steak à Viriato)

Yet another recipe from the Estalagem Viriato: grilled steak, but typically Portuguese in the way it is served.

Serves four

1 lb. carrots, finely sliced	6 oz. Patna rice
knob of butter	1 tablespoon olive oil
1 lump sugar	1½ lb. rump steak
seasoning	cooking oil

Cook the carrots gently until tender in 5 tablespoons of water, a knob of butter, a lump of sugar and seasoning.

Cook the rice in boiling salted water for 12 minutes. Drain and, while still warm, stir in the olive oil.

Brush the meat with the cooking oil. Season and grill according to taste.

Serve with the rice and the carrots and with potato crisps.

Bifes na frigideira
(Fried Steak)

Serves four

2 tablespoons olive oil	seasoning
2 oz. butter	¼ lb. *presunto* (see p. 18) *or*
6 cloves garlic, crushed	ham, chopped
1 bay leaf	3 dessertspoons dry port
1¼ lb. steak, in 4 portions	1 lemon, cut into quarters

Heat the oil and butter in a *frigideira* or large frying pan with the garlic and the bay leaf. Season the steaks, put them in the pan and cook according to taste. Remove and keep warm.

Add the ham and the wine to the pan and cook gently until heated through. Pour over the steaks, and serve with lemon quarters and fried potatoes.

Carneiro recheado à Portuguesa
(Portuguese Stuffed Lamb)

Serves four

1 oz. butter	1 teaspoon fresh chopped
1 large onion, chopped	coriander
2 oz. shelled almonds,	seasoning
chopped	grated rind of half a lemon
2 oz. green olives, stoned and	1 egg
chopped	1 boned loin of lamb, about
½ cup wholewheat breadcrumbs	2 lb.
	1 glass white wine

Melt the butter and cook the onion until soft. Add the almonds, olives, breadcrumbs, coriander, seasoning and lemon rind. Beat the egg and add to the mixture. Spread the mixture over the meat, roll up and fasten with string. Season, put in a baking dish and pour the wine over it. Cook in a moderate oven (350° F., gas 4) until tender, about 45 to 60 minutes, basting occasionally.

Chanfana
(Braised Leg of Lamb)

The recipe below won first prize in a national competition for Portuguese cookery and confectionery.

Serves six

1 leg lamb, about 4 lb.	1 dessertspoon chopped
¼ lb. bacon, chopped	parsley
2 onions, sliced	½ teaspoon paprika
3 cloves of garlic, crushed	¼ teaspoon grated nutmeg
1 oz. butter	seasoning
1 tablespoon olive oil	a good ¼ pint red wine
2 bay leaves	

Place the joint in a casserole, cover it with a mixture of all the other ingredients, except the wine, and leave for an hour. Then pour the wine over it, cover and cook in a hot oven (400° F., gas 6) for about 2 hours, until it is done. During the cooking add a little more wine if necessary.

Carve the joint and serve with the sauce spooned over it and with potatoes in the Portuguese manner, i.e. boiled in salted water and peeled after they are cooked.

Carneiro à Transmontana
(Transmontana Lamb)

Serves six

1 leg of lamb	1 fl. oz. stock
seasoning	1 onion, sliced
1 oz. butter	2 eggs, beaten
4 cloves garlic, crushed	breadcrumbs
1 fl. oz. dry white wine	

Place the meat in a baking dish, rub well with the seasoning and cover with the butter and garlic. Pour the wine and stock over it and add the sliced onion. Roast in a moderate oven (350° F., gas 4) for 1¾–2 hours, basting occasionally.

Remove from the oven, cover with the beaten eggs and sprinkle with breadcrumbs. Return to the oven and brown quickly.

Take out of the oven, allow to get cold and slice.

Costeletas de carneiro à Escondidinho
(Lamb Chops Escondidinho)

Serves four

4 lamb chops	1 teaspoon Worcester sauce
seasoning	1 tablespoon dry port
2 oz. butter	1 tablespoon cream
1 teaspoon French mustard	

Prepare the chops, season and fry in the butter. When well browned on both sides, put in a dish and keep warm. Put the mustard, Worcester sauce and port into a pan and heat gently, quickly add the cream and pour over the chops. Serve with fried potatoes and a green salad.

Maranhos à Beira Baixa
(Mint-flavoured Lamb and Rice)

The recipe I was given for this dish started: 'Wash a sheep's craw, thoroughly scrape inside and cut it into 3–4 pieces.' I felt that a sheep's craw was, to say the least of it, difficult to come by, so I have simplified and anglicized this recipe. Even in its simpler form it is delicious, with its strong fresh taste of mint.

Serves four

1 lb. lean, boneless lamb, cut into small pieces
¼ lb. *presunto* (see p. 18) *or* ham, finely chopped
¼ lb. *chouriço* (see p. 18) *or* garlic sausage, finely chopped
¾ pint dry white wine

3 handfuls fresh mint, chopped
1 clove garlic, crushed
seasoning
1 tablespoon olive oil
½ lb. Patna rice
½ pint water

Put all the meat into a dish and add the wine, mint, garlic and seasoning. Cover and leave in a cool place overnight.

Drain the meat, reserving the marinade. Heat the oil in a saucepan, add the meat and lightly brown over a gentle heat. Remove the saucepan from the heat and add the rice, marinade and water. Put the mixture in a greased pudding basin, big enough to allow for swelling. Cover with foil and steam until the rice and meat are tender, 1½–2 hours.

Iscas
(Lisbon Liver)

Serves four

2 fl. oz. dry white wine
2 tablespoons wine vinegar
5 cloves garlic, crushed
1 bay leaf
seasoning

1½ lb. lamb's liver, thinly sliced
olive oil
2 oz. bacon, chopped

Make a marinade with the wine, vinegar, garlic, bay leaf and seasoning, pour it over the liver, cover and leave for 24 hours.

Take out the liver and pat dry. Reserve the marinade. Heat in a frying pan sufficient oil to cover the bottom of the pan, add the liver and the bacon, and cook until tender over moderate heat, turning the liver once. Remove the meat and keep warm. Add the marinade to the pan, taking out the bay leaf, and reduce quickly. Pour it over the meat and serve, accompanied by fried sliced potatoes.

Lingua de vaca à Portuguesa
(Portuguese Ox Tongue)

Serves six

1 salted ox tongue	3 fl. oz. Madeira (sherry can
1 oz. butter	be used)
4 medium-sized ripe tomatoes,	1 dessertspoon white wine
peeled and chopped	vinegar
3 pickled cucumbers, sliced	seasoning
½ pint beef stock	1 dessertspoon flour

Soak the tongue in cold water for 4 hours, to remove the salt, changing the water once or twice. Then put it in a large saucepan and add enough cold water to cover. Cover the pan and simmer over gentle heat for 4 hours.

Lift out from the pan and with a sharp knife carefully remove the skin and any bones and gristle.

Melt the butter in a large, heavy, oven-proof casserole and in it gently brown the tongue on all sides. Add the tomatoes, cucumbers, stock, Madeira (or sherry), vinegar and seasoning. Cover and bake in a moderate oven (350° F., gas 4) until the tongue is fully cooked, about 30–45 minutes.

Remove the tongue to a serving dish. To the casserole add the flour, previously mixed with a little of the liquid, and cook gently until slightly thickened. Serve the tongue surrounded by the mixture from the casserole.

This dish may be accompanied by *molho de azeda* (see p. 89).

Lombinhos de porco
(Loin of Pork Slices)

Serves four

4 slices of lean pork loin	1 sprig parsley, chopped
4 fl. oz. dry white wine	seasoning
1 bay leaf	oil for frying
1 clove garlic, crushed	

Place the slices of pork in a dish. Make a marinade with the wine, bay leaf, garlic, parsley and seasoning and pour it over. Cover and leave for 4 hours.

Remove the meat from the marinade and pat dry. Heat the oil in a large frying pan and add the meat. Lightly brown on both sides, then add a little of the marinade and cook over moderate heat until the meat is tender, about 10 minutes.

Serve with fried potatoes and with creamed spinach, to which a tablespoon of Parmesan cheese has been added.

Lombo de porco à moda do Alentejo
(Alentejo Pork Fillet)

Serves four

4 slices of pork fillet	1 bay leaf
3 fl. oz. dry white wine	salt
1 fl. oz. water	1 dessertspoon paprika
2 cloves garlic, crushed	2 onions, chopped
juice of one orange	1 orange cut into quarters

Put the meat in a casserole, cover with a marinade made of the wine, water, garlic, orange juice, bay leaf and seasoning and leave overnight.

Sprinkle the chopped onion over the meat, cover and cook in a moderate oven (350° F., gas 4) until the meat is tender, about 40–60 minutes.

Serve with fried potatoes and garnish with orange quarters.

Porco com amêijoas à Alentejana
(Pork with Clams)

Clams should be used in this recipe to give the true flavour, but if these are unobtainable mussels can be used instead.

Serves four

1½ lb. lean, boneless pork	2 onions, sliced
½ pint dry white wine	4 medium-sized tomatoes,
2 heaped teaspoons paprika	chopped
1 bay leaf	2 lb. clams in their shells
2 cloves	chopped coriander
seasoning	chopped parsley
5 cloves garlic	1 lemon
2 oz. lard	

Cut the meat into 1-inch cubes. Put in a dish and add the wine, paprika, bay leaf, cloves, seasoning and 3 cloves of garlic, crushed. Cover and leave overnight, turning occasionally.

In a large saucepan heat 1 oz. lard, add the onions, the tomatoes and the rest of the garlic, crushed, and cook gently until the onions are soft. Season.

Wash the clams very thoroughly in several waters, scraping off any barnacles from the shells. Discard any which remain open, as this shows that they are dead. Put them in a saucepan with the onion mixture, cover and cook hard until all are open, about 5 minutes, then cook for a further minute.

Meanwhile drain the pork, keeping the marinade.

Heat the rest of the lard in a large frying pan, add the pork and brown on all sides over medium heat. Add the marinade and continue to cook uncovered until there is very little liquid.

Serve the pork, the clams in their shells and the onion mixture with some boiled potatoes, sprinkling everything with coriander and parsley and garnishing with lemon quarters.

Rojões à moda do Minho
(Pork in the Minho Style)

Serves four

3 fl. oz. dry white wine	seasoning
1 tablespoon lemon juice	2 lb. lean pork, cut in cubes
1 dessertspoon ground cumin	1 oz. lard
3 cloves garlic, crushed	olives and lemon quarters for
1 bay leaf	garnishing

Make a marinade with the wine, lemon juice, cumin, garlic, bay leaf and seasoning. Put the pork in a dish, cover with the marinade and leave overnight.

Remove the meat and pat dry, reserving the marinade. Melt the lard in a heavy casserole, add the meat and brown slowly on all sides. Add the marinade, cover and cook over gentle heat until the meat is tender, about 45 minutes.

Serve with fried sliced potatoes and garnished with lemon quarters and olives.

Leitão assado
(Roast Sucking Pig)

Serves six to eight

1 oz. butter	1 sucking pig, with some of
½ lb. calf's or pig's liver	the blood
2 onions, sliced	2 tablespoons flour
2 tomatoes, sliced	2 egg yolks
1 sprig parsley, chopped	seasoning
1 slice ham, chopped	olive oil
4 oz. stoned black olives	

Melt the butter in a pan, add the liver, chopped, and cook until lightly browned. Remove and keep warm. Put in the onions and fry gently until golden. Add the tomatoes and parsley and cook for 5 minutes. Return the liver to the pan, together with the ham, the olives and the blood. Mix the flour with enough cold water to make a smooth, thin paste, beat in the egg yolks and add to the mixture in the pan. Cook over gentle heat for 10 minutes, stirring frequently, and season to taste.

Stuff the pig with the mixture, sew up the opening with strong cotton, season and brush the outside with a little olive oil. Place in a baking dish, covering the ears with foil, and roast in a moderate oven (350° F., gas 4) until tender (about 2 hours), basting from time to time.

Tripas à moda do Porto
(Porto Style Tripe)

Gastronomically, Oporto is as famous for its *tripas à moda do Porto* as Lisbon is for its *iscas*. It is also well known as the city where people enjoy good food and are accustomed to eating very large meals. This has led to the custom of serving half-portions, which is really a misnomer as one portion is usually quite large enough for two. When eating in Oporto, therefore, it is as well to remember this habit; I think you will find a half portion quite a large meal.

The basic method for cooking *tripas à moda do Porto* is always the same, but some of the ingredients vary. One recipe I was given included a pig's ear and a large piece of pig's head. In this recipe I have slightly simplified the ingredients and the cooking and tried to make it easier for the cook in this country.

Serves four

1 lb. tripe	2 carrots, thinly sliced
1 calf's foot *or* 1 gammon bone	3 medium onions, sliced
seasoning	1 oz. lard
5 oz. dried haricot beans, previously soaked for at least 24 hours	3 teaspoons ground cumin
	1 small handful parsley, chopped
3 oz. ham	1 bay leaf
6 oz. *chouriço* (see p. 18) *or* garlic sausage	cooked Patna rice

Wash the tripe well in cold water. Cut into smallish pieces and put in a saucepan with the calf's foot or gammon bone and just enough salted water to cover. Cover, bring to the boil and simmer until the tripe is cooked, 2½–3 hours. Drain.

In another pan cook the beans, again with just enough water to cover, until they are tender, about an hour. Drain.

Cut up the ham and the *chouriço* or garlic sausage and put them in a saucepan together with the carrots and one onion. Season and cover with water and cook until the carrots are tender, about 15 minutes. Drain, saving ½ a pint of the broth.

Melt the lard in a casserole and cook the rest of the onions, sprinkled with the cumin, until soft. Add the broth and all the other ingredients except the bone and the rice, season and simmer for a further 30 minutes.

Serve with the rice.

Dobrada

(Tripe with Chick Peas)

Serves four

¾ lb. chick peas
salt
1½ lb. tripe
1 sprig of parsley
6 peppercorns
6 cloves
1½ oz. lard
1 medium-sized onion, sliced

1 stick celery, sliced in
    matchstick-size pieces
2 tomatoes, sliced
1 clove garlic, crushed
1 tablespoon oil
¼ lb. *linguiça* (see p. 18) *or*
    garlic sausage, sliced

Soak the chick peas in cold water overnight, then cook them in a saucepan in plenty of salted water until tender, about 2–3 hours. Drain.

Wash the tripe thoroughly, then put it in a saucepan with plenty of salted water, the parsley, peppercorns and cloves, and simmer gently until tender, about 2 hours. Drain.

Melt the lard in a casserole and add the onion and celery. Cook gently until soft, then add the tomatoes and garlic. Cook for a further five minutes, then add the tripe and chick peas.

Heat the oil in a frying pan and lightly fry the sausage.

Serve the *dobrada* in the casserole, garnished with the sausage, and with sliced boiled carrots and potatoes.

Mãos de vitela à jardineira
(Veal Trotter Stew)

Mãos means 'hands', and in this recipe refers to the trotters. I have given pig's trotters as an alternative to the veal used in the original recipe, as pig's trotters are more readily available in this country.

Serves four

2 veal or pig's trotters with
   the hocks
2 pints water
1 large onion, sliced
1 handful parsley, chopped
1 bay leaf
6 peppercorns
salt

1 oz. lard
3 tablespoons vinegar
½ lb. shelled peas
4 carrots, sliced
2 turnips, chopped
1 knob of butter
squeeze of lemon juice

Wash, clean and trim the trotters and hocks.

In a large saucepan bring the water to the boil. Add the trotters and hocks, the onion, parsley, bay leaf, peppercorns, salt, lard and 2 tablespoons vinegar. Cover and simmer gently for about 2 hours, until the meat is tender.

Meanwhile cook the peas, carrots and turnips until tender and drain.

When the meat is cooked, remove from the saucepan, keeping the stock. Take all the meat off the bones and cut it up into small pieces. Strain the stock and reduce it considerably by boiling hard for several minutes.

Add to the vegetables a knob of butter, a squeeze of lemon juice and 1 tablespoon vinegar. Mix in the meat.

Serve on a large plate and hand round the stock as a gravy.

Frango na púcara
(Chicken Casserole)

A *púcara* is a deep earthenware pot with a lid.

Serves four

1 medium-sized chicken

1 slice *presunto* (see p. 18) *or* ham, chopped

4 medium-sized onions, sliced

2 tomatoes, chopped

2 cloves garlic, crushed

2 oz. butter

1 bay leaf

1 tablespoon French mustard seasoning

2 wine glasses dry port

1 wine glass dry white wine

Prepare the chicken in the usual way and put it in a casserole together with the other ingredients. Cover and cook in a moderate oven (350° F., gas 4) until the chicken is cooked, about 1 hour. Serve with fried potatoes.

Frango à Beira Alta

(Beira Alta Chicken)

Serves six

1 4 lb. chicken

2 thin slices *presunto* (see p. 18) *or* ham
seasoning

6 oz. cottage cheese

2 oz. butter

1½ lb. small new scraped potatoes

Ease up the skin on the breast of the chicken and insert the *presunto* or ham. Season the inside. Mix the cheese with 1 oz. butter and some black pepper, spoon the mixture into the cavity of the bird and sew up the opening. Place in a baking dish, surrounded by the potatoes, and brush both chicken and potatoes with 1 oz. melted butter. Cook in a moderate oven (350° F., gas 4) for about 1½ hours, basting occasionally. Serve with a green salad.

Frangos no espeto à minha moda

(Chicken Grilled on a Spit)

In this recipe the chicken is covered with *piri-piri* and melted butter and grilled on a spit. *Piri-piri* is a hot chilli sauce which I have described, together with the method of making it, on p. 18. However, tabasco sauce can be used with almost the same result.

If you do not have a spit, the chicken can be roasted instead. It must then be basted and turned occasionally, in order to cover it with the sauce and brown it on all sides.

Serves six

1 chicken, about 4½ lb.	1 tablespoon melted butter
1 sprig parsley	2 tablespoons *piri-piri*
salt	1 clove garlic, crushed
lemon juice	

Wipe the chicken over with a damp cloth. Put the parsley inside, rub the outside with salt and sprinkle with lemon juice. Leave for 1 hour.

Place the chicken in a baking tray and cook in a moderate oven (350° F., gas 4) for 1 hour. Remove from the oven and brush with a mixture of the melted butter, the *piri-piri* and the garlic. Then either grill on a spit or roast in a hot oven (400° F., gas 7), turning and basting occasionally, until it is cooked and the skin is crisp and golden, about 15 minutes.

Frango com ervilhas à Portuguesa
(Chicken with Peas)

Serves four

2 tablespoons olive oil	6 fl. oz. chicken stock
1 oz. butter	2 fl. oz. dry madeira or dry
1 medium-sized onion, sliced	port
1 chicken, about 2½ lb.	seasoning
trussed	1 lb. shelled peas

Heat the oil and the butter in a heavy casserole, add the onion and cook gently until limp. Remove and keep warm.

Put the chicken in the casserole and lightly brown on all sides. Add the onion, stock and wine and season to taste. Cover and cook over gentle heat until the chicken is tender, about 1 hour. Ten minutes before the chicken is ready add the peas.

This dish is very good accompanied by *batatas estufadas à Portuguesa* (see p. 87).

Coelho à cacadora
(Hunter's Rabbit)

Serves four

1 rabbit	1 oz. butter
6 oz. dry white wine	2 tablespoons olive oil
2 tablespoons white wine vinegar	4 medium-sized onions, sliced
1 bay leaf	1 oz. chopped bacon
1 clove garlic, crushed	¼ lb. mushrooms, sliced
seasoning	1 sprig parsley, chopped
	1 sprig coriander, chopped

Cut the rabbit into serving pieces. Make a marinade of the wine, vinegar, bay leaf, garlic and seasoning. Put the rabbit pieces in the marinade and leave overnight. Remove from the marinade and dry.

Heat the butter and the oil in a casserole and in it lightly brown the rabbit pieces. Remove them and keep them warm. Cook the onions, bacon and mushrooms in the casserole until the onions are soft.

Put back the rabbit pieces and pour over the marinade, after removing the bay leaf and adding the parsley and coriander. Cook in a moderate oven (350° F., gas 4) until the rabbit is tender, about half to three quarters of an hour, basting occasionally.

Coelho com vinho do porto
(Rabbit in Port Wine)

Serves four

2 oz. butter	1 sprig of tarragon
4 onions, sliced	¼ teaspoon grated nutmeg
2 oz. mushrooms, sliced	seasoning
¼ lb. ham, chopped	1 rabbit
1 bay leaf	2 carrots, sliced
2 cloves of garlic, crushed	1 wine glass white wine
1 sprig of thyme	1 wine glass port

In a saucepan melt 1 oz. butter, put in 2 of the onions, the mushrooms, ham, bay leaf, garlic, thyme, tarragon, grated nutmeg, pepper and salt. Cook gently until the onions are limp. Stuff the rabbit with this mixture and sew up the opening.

Melt the rest of the butter in a casserole, put in the carrots, the other onions and the rabbit and brown lightly. Add the wine.

Cover and cook in a moderate oven (350° F., gas 4), basting occasionally, until the rabbit is tender, about 2 hours.

Perdizes com nozes
(Partridges with Nuts)

Serves four

8 fl. oz. dry white wine	4 partridges
2 fl. oz. olive oil	1 oz. butter
juice of half a lemon	¼ lb. bacon
1 carrot, grated	6 shallots, sliced
1 onion, sliced	1 wineglass brandy
1 bay leaf	4 slices of bread, with the
1 sprig thyme, chopped	crusts removed
seasoning	2 oz. walnuts, chopped

Make a marinade with the wine, oil, lemon juice, grated carrot, onion, bay leaf, thyme and seasoning. Place the partridges in a dish, pour the marinade over them, cover and leave for 12 hours. Remove the birds and pat dry. Strain and keep the marinade.

Melt the butter over low heat in a heavy casserole. Cut the bacon into small pieces and cook gently in the butter. Add the shallots and the partridges and lightly brown the birds. Cover and cook over low heat until the birds are tender, about 20 minutes. Remove the casserole from the heat, pour the brandy over the birds and set it alight.

Toast the bread, place each partridge on a piece of toast, scatter the walnuts over them and keep warm.

Add the marinade to the gravy in the casserole, quickly reduce to a thin sauce and serve with the birds.

Perdiz fria à moda de Coimbra
(Cold Partridge Coimbra Style)

Serves four

4 fl. oz. olive oil	4 peppercorns
2 large onions, sliced	salt
4 partridges	4 fl. oz. dry white wine
4 cloves	2 fl. oz. white wine vinegar
1 teaspoon cumin	

Heat the oil in a large casserole and lightly brown the onions and the birds. Add all the other ingredients, cover and cook over low heat until the birds are tender, about 30 minutes.

Remove from the heat. Place the birds on a serving dish. Strain the gravy and pour it over them. Serve cold with fried or boiled potatoes.

Folar de valpaços
(Easter Pie)

Serves four

6 oz. flour	2 chicken pieces, about 7–8 oz.
½ teaspoon salt	altogether, boned, skinned
¼ oz. yeast	and chopped
½ teaspoon sugar	6 oz. lean pork, chopped
½ oz. butter	6 oz. *presunto* (see p. 18) *or*
½ oz. lard	ham, chopped
1 dessertspoon olive oil	6 oz. *chouriço* (see p. 18) *or*
2 eggs	garlic sausage, chopped
seasoning	1 egg yolk, beaten

Warm a large mixing bowl and into it sieve the flour and salt. Make a hole in the middle. Cream the yeast and sugar and add a tablespoon of warm water. Melt the fats in a pan with the oil. Pour the yeast and sugar into the middle of the flour and mix by turning the outside into the centre. Add the eggs one by one, mixing well, and finally the melted fats and oil. Stir the mixture until it comes away from the sides of the bowl. Put the bowl in a warm place, cover with a cloth and leave until the mixture has risen, about 30 minutes. Turn the dough out on to a floured board and knead. Put back into a floured bowl, cover again with a cloth and leave in a warm place for 1½ hours.

Grease a baking tin about 3 inches in depth. Divide the dough into 3 portions. On a floured board roll out one portion of the dough and with it line the tin. Mix and season all the meats and spread half over the dough in the tin. Roll out a second portion of dough and with it cover the meat. Spread the rest of the meat over it and cover with the rolled out final portion of dough. Leave in a warm place for about 20 minutes to rise. Brush the surface with the beaten egg yolk and cook in a hot oven (400° F., gas 7) for 45 minutes.

Empadas de galinha à moda do Alentejo
(Chicken Pies, Alentejo Style)

Serves six

1 chicken, about 3 lb.	salt
1 oz. *touchinho* (see p. 18) *or* bacon	5 egg yolks
	lemon juice
1 sprig parsley, chopped	grated nutmeg
1 onion, peeled and studded with cloves	8 oz. flour
	3 oz. butter
1 fl. oz. wine vinegar	3 oz. lard
4 peppercorns	

Cut the chicken into joints and put them in a large saucepan with the bacon, parsley, onion, vinegar, peppercorns and salt and enough water just to cover. Cover the pan, bring to the boil and simmer until the meat is cooked, about 45–60 minutes.

Take out the chicken and bacon. Strain and reserve the stock. Remove skin and bones from the chicken and cut the meat and the bacon into small pieces. Place in a dish.

Beat 4 of the egg yolks and gradually add 8 fl. oz. of the warm broth. Heat the mixture gently in a saucepan, stirring continuously, until it thickens slightly. Do not allow to boil. Add a good squeeze of lemon juice, sprinkle with grated nutmeg and pour over the meat. Cover the dish, chill and leave overnight.

Next day sieve the flour and a good pinch of salt into a bowl, rub in the fat until the mixture resembles fine breadcrumbs and add just enough cold water to make a soft dough.

Roll out on a floured board. Cut 6 circles of pastry, line 6 small greased pasty tins with them and fill with the chicken mixture. From the rest of the pastry cut 6 slightly smaller circles and cover the pies. Seal the edges and cut a vent in each. Beat the remaining egg yolk and with it brush the tops.

Bake in a hot oven (450° F., gas 8) until cooked and golden, about 20–25 minutes.

Arroz com figado de vitela à Lisboeta
(Rice with Calf's Liver, Lisbon Style)

Serves four

arroz de manteiga (see p. 92)
3½ oz. butter
1 medium onion, sliced
seasoning

1 lb. calf's (or lamb's) liver,
  sliced
1 sprig parsley, chopped

Prepare the *arroz de manteiga*.

Heat ½ oz. of the butter in a small frying pan, add the onion and cook gently until limp and golden. Keep warm.

Season the liver. Heat the rest of the butter in a large frying pan, put in the liver with the parsley and fry quickly, turning once. Add the onions and remove from the heat.

To serve, make a border of the rice round a large serving dish and place the liver with the onions and parsley in the centre.

Arroz de pato à moda de Braga
(Duck and Rice in Braga Style)

Serves six

1 duck, about 5 lb.
½ lb. *presunto* (see p. 18) *or*
  ham, chopped
½ lb. *chouriço* (see p. 18) *or*
  garlic sausage, chopped
1 onion, sliced

1 bay leaf
6 peppercorns
salt
1 lb. Patna rice
1 orange

Place the duck in a casserole and add the ham, sausage, onion, bay leaf, peppercorns and salt. Just cover with water. Put the casserole in a moderate oven (350° F., gas 4) and cook for 1½–2 hours, until the bird is tender. Put it on a serving dish and keep hot.

Strain the stock into a saucepan, keeping the meat and onion but discarding the bay leaf and peppercorns. Reheat it and when it is boiling add the rice and boil for about 8 minutes, until the rice is nearly cooked. Strain. Put the rice into the casserole and add the sausage, ham and onion. Bake in a moderate oven until the rice is fully cooked.

Carve the duck. Serve it with the rice mixture from the casserole and garnished with orange segments.

Frango com arroz

(Chicken with Rice)

Serves four

1½ oz. butter	1 chicken, about 2½ lb. trussed
salt	juice of half a lemon
ground black pepper	*arroz de manteiga* (see p. 92)

Melt the butter in a heavy casserole. Season the chicken, put it in the casserole and sprinkle with the lemon juice. Cover and cook in a moderate oven (350° F., gas 4) until tender, about 1 hour.

Meanwhile prepare the *arroz de manteiga* and keep hot.

Remove the chicken and cut into portions. Put the rice on a serving dish and place the chicken portions on top.

Serve with a green salad.

Arroz de Espinho

(Espinho Rice)

Serves four

1 lb. veal, cut into smallish pieces	1 sprig parsley, chopped
	seasoning
4 oz. *chouriço* (see p. 18) *or* garlic sausage, chopped	1 tablespoon lemon juice
	1 pint chicken stock
2 oz. *presunto* (see p. 18) *or* ham, chopped	half a white cabbage, cored and sliced
2 carrots, sliced	½ lb. Patna rice
1 medium onion, sliced	1 lemon, cut into quarters
½ oz. lard	

Put all the meat and the carrots, onion, lard, parsley, seasoning, lemon juice and stock into a saucepan, cover and simmer over gentle heat for 2 hours.

Then in another saucepan put the cabbage in boiling salted water, cover and cook for 3 minutes. Drain and add to the meat mixture together with the washed rice. Cover and cook over gentle heat until the rice is tender and all the liquid has been absorbed, about 30 minutes.

Serve garnished with the lemon quarters.

Arroz d'Algarve
(Algarve Rice)

Serves four

2 tablespoons olive oil	10 oz. long-grain rice
6 oz. lean pork, cut into small pieces	1 pint chicken stock
1 large onion, chopped	2 tablespoons lemon juice
¾ lb. ham, diced	seasoning
¾ lb. *chouriço* (see p. 18) *or* garlic sausage, diced	1 lemon

Heat the olive oil in a heavy casserole, lightly brown the pork and cook the onion until soft. Add the ham, sausage and rice and cook for a few minutes, then add the stock and lemon juice. Cook in a moderate oven (350° F., gas 4) for about 30 minutes, until the rice is cooked and the meat tender. Season if necessary and serve with a lemon quarter for each person.

Feijoada à Algarvia
com macarronete cortado
(Macaroni with Beans in the Algarve Style)

Serves four

4 oz. black-eyed or haricot beans	1 large onion, sliced
6 oz. salt pork *or* gammon	1 tablespoon olive oil
6 oz. *morcela* (see p. 18) *or* black pudding, sliced	seasoning
1 teaspoon ground cumin (if black pudding is used)	1 small head of white cabbage, cut into strips
	4 oz. short cut macaroni

Soak the beans and the pork in cold water overnight.

Cut the pork into cubes and put it in a casserole with the beans, black pudding, cumin, onion, oil, seasoning and water almost to cover. Cover and cook in a moderate oven (350° F., gas 4) until the beans are tender, about 30 minutes. Add the cabbage and a little more water if there is not enough to cook it, but do not make the mixture too wet. Cook for approximately 15 minutes in a moderate oven until the cabbage is tender but still crisp.

Meanwhile cook the macaroni in plenty of salted water for 10 minutes. Drain and add to the mixture in the casserole and serve.

Favas guisadas com paio e chouriço
(Broad Bean Stew with Smoked Pork and Garlic Sausage)

Serves four

1 tablespoon olive oil
1 piece of fat bacon, chopped
1 onion, sliced
2 lb. shelled broad beans
¼ lb. *chouriço* (see p. 18) *or* garlic sausage, chopped
¼ lb. *paio* (see p. 18) *or* smoked ham sausage, chopped

1 slice ham, chopped
1 clove garlic, crushed
1 sprig coriander, chopped
1 bay leaf
10 fl. oz. water
seasoning

Heat the oil in a heavy casserole over gentle heat, add the bacon and the onion and cook until the onion is soft and the bacon crisp. Then add the other ingredients and cook over low heat until the beans are tender, about 10 minutes.

Feijão frade com chouriço
(Dried Beans with Sausage)

Serves four

½ lb. black-eyed or haricot beans
3 oz. butter
nutmeg
seasoning

3–4 oz. double cream
lemon juice
2 stalks celery, thinly sliced
6 oz. *chouriço* (see p. 18) *or* garlic sausage, diced

Soak the beans overnight. Drain and put them in a pan with just enough water to cover. Add 2 oz. butter and some grated nutmeg and cook without a lid over low heat for about an hour, until the beans are quite cooked. Add more water if the mixture becomes too dry. Add some salt and pepper just before the beans are cooked. The liquid should be considerably reduced. Stir in the cream and a good squeeze of lemon juice, and keep warm. Heat the rest of the butter in a small frying pan. Put in the celery and the sausage. Fry gently until lightly browned. Fold into the bean mixture and serve.

Favas com touchinho
(Beans with Pork)

The beans known as *favas* in the Iberian peninsular are the same as our broad beans. They are used a great deal in the cookery of both Portugal and Spain. *Favas com touchinho* is a favourite dish of the Portuguese. This recipe is a variation containing *morcela* sausage.

Serves four

¼ lb. *touchinho* (see p. 18) *or* fat pork
3 tablespoons olive oil
2 large onions, sliced
¼ lb. *morcela* (see p. 18) *or* black pudding
3 lb. shelled broad beans
2 cloves garlic, crushed
1 handful fresh coriander, chopped
2 teaspoons ground cumin (if black pudding is used)
seasoning
1 teaspoon sugar
8 fl. oz. broth

Cut the pork into medium-sized pieces. Heat the oil in a heavy casserole, add the pork and lightly brown on all sides. Add the onions and cook until soft. Then put in the *morcela*, cut into small slices, and stir to prevent sticking until it is fried. Add the rest of the ingredients, cover and cook in a medium oven (350° F., gas 4) until the beans are tender, about 30 minutes. Serve with a lettuce salad.

Egg Dishes

Omelete com tomate e arroz à Portuguesa
(Omelette with Tomato and Rice)

Generally in Portugal, omelettes are not stuffed, but the accompaniments are placed round them.

Serves four

arroz de manteiga (see p. 92)
using 6 oz. rice, 1 medium
onion, 2½ oz. butter and
¾ pint stock

tomatada à Portuguesa (see
p. 89) using ½ lb. tomatoes,
1 medium onion and 3
tablespoons olive oil
8 eggs
butter
seasoning

Prepare the *arroz de manteiga* and the *tomatada à Portuguesa*.

With the eggs, butter and seasoning make either one or two omelettes in the usual way.

To serve, place the omelette in the centre of a large dish and on one side put the *arroz de manteiga* and on the other the *tomatada à Portuguesa*.

Omelette Albufeirense

Serves two

½ lb. cooked sliced potatoes	2 oz. *chouriço* (see p. 18) *or*
olive oil	garlic sausage, sliced
4 eggs	2 oz. black olives
seasoning	tomato quarters
1 oz. butter	cucumber slices

Lightly fry the potatoes in a little olive oil. Beat the eggs with the seasoning, add to the hot melted butter and cook the omelette in the usual way. Serve with the fried potatoes, sausage, olives, tomato quarters and cucumber slices.

Ovos mexidos de cebolada à moda de Coimbra

(Scrambled Eggs with Onion, Coimbra Style)

Coimbra is the university city of Portugal. It has a commanding position high above the Mondego river. The road to it from Penacova is beautiful, following the line of the river through steep hills, many dotted with small villages, the houses appearing to cling to the slopes. The river is wide, but once when we saw it after a six-months' drought there was very little water and the pebbly river bed was almost completely exposed. The village women do their washing in the river and even in wetter summers the river bed is bright and colourful with the clothes flapping gaily from lines and poles or laid out on the shingle to dry.

There are two quite distinct parts of the city of Coimbra, the busy modern commercial district with a handsome tree-lined avenue bordering the river and the old city on the hill behind and above it. The latter is dominated by the university buildings, up to which climb numerous tortuous cobbled streets and lanes, many only suitable for pedestrians; among them stands the old cathedral, which was built on the site of the mosque of the time of the Moorish occupation. It is fascinating to wander round this area, and the sudden change of atmosphere from the bustling life of the lower town is very striking.

From Coimbra comes this simple variation of scrambled eggs.

Serves four

2 oz. butter	4 tablespoons bread cubes
4 large onions, sliced	8 eggs
oil for frying	seasoning

Heat the butter in a large frying pan, add the onions and cook gently until limp and golden.

Meanwhile in a small frying pan heat the oil and lightly fry the bread cubes, turning on all sides. Drain and keep warm.

Beat the eggs with the seasoning and add to the onions in the pan. Stir with a wooden spoon until the desired consistency is reached. Add the fried bread cubes and serve immediately.

Ovos com ervilhas

(Eggs with Peas)

This is a popular dish throughout Portugal, both for lunch and for dinner.

Serves four

2 oz. butter	3 fl. oz. water
1 lb. shelled peas	salt
12 very small whole onions, skinned	ground black pepper
1 sprig parsley, chopped	8 eggs

Melt the butter in a heavy casserole over gentle heat. Add the peas, onions, parsley and water and season to taste. Cover and cook gently until the peas are tender.

With the back of a tablespoon make eight depressions in the mixture and into each break an egg. Sprinkle the tops of the eggs with a little salt and pepper, cover the casserole and cook again over gentle heat until the eggs are done, according to taste, but for not less than 10 minutes.

Vegetables and Salads

The vegetables grown in Portugal are generally those which are grown in this country, but they are sometimes served differently.

Peas and beans are great favourites, but are seldom served on their own. Peas may be stewed and flavoured with herbs or combined with rice. Beans, both fresh and dried, are frequently used with onions and tomatoes. Chick peas, which are not grown in this country but can now be bought from many shops, are cooked with other vegetables, such as spinach, and are served particularly as an accompaniment to *bacalhau*.

Turnips appear on Portuguese menus, but it is the tops rather than the roots which are used.

As in this country, potatoes accompany most meat and fish dishes, except when rice is served. They may be fried, but otherwise they are always boiled in their skins and peeled after they are cooked.

Salads are served at almost every meal, whether hot or cold. Lettuce may be combined with watercress to give a sharp taste, or sprinkled with chopped coriander. Tomatoes with sliced onions are popular. The tomatoes, however, are quite different from ours, being large, irregular in shape and varying in colour from orange-red to yellow and almost green; not as attractive to look at, but with a wonderful flavour.

The markets in Portugal are always worth a visit, and the fruit and vegetable stalls are particularly colourful. One thing I found, which I have never seen before, is that mixed salad greens, lettuce with herbs and sometimes watercress, are all combined and sold as a salad; a good idea which I think might be adopted in this country.

Ervilhas guisadas à Portuguesa
(Stewed Peas)

Serves four

1 oz. butter	1 sprig parsley, chopped
1 oz. lard	1 sprig coriander, chopped
1 medium onion, sliced	seasoning
3 tablespoons chicken stock	1 lb. shelled peas

Melt the fats in a heavy saucepan, add the onion, and cook over gentle heat until limp and golden. Remove from the heat, add the stock, parsley and coriander, and season to taste. Return to the heat and when the liquid is boiling add the peas, cover, and cook over gentle heat until tender.

Feijão frade guisado à Portuguesa
(Haricot Bean Stew)

Serves four

½ lb. haricot beans	1 lb. *touchinho* (see p. 18) cut
2 pints water	into cubes
1 medium onion, sliced	*tomatada à Portuguesa* (see
1 sprig parsley, chopped	p. 89)
seasoning	

Soak the beans overnight. Drain and put in a saucepan with the water, onion, parsley and seasoning. Cover and cook over gentle heat for half an hour. Add the *touchinho* and continue to simmer until both beans and *touchinho* are cooked, about half an hour to one hour. Drain and serve with the *tomatada* poured over.

This dish can be made more substantial by the addition of one poached egg per person on the top of the mixture before the *tomatada* is poured over.

Grão com tomatada
(Chick Peas with Tomato Pulp)

Serves four

10 oz. chick peas   *tomatada* (see p. 89)

Soak the chick peas for 24 hours.

The next day put them in a saucepan with plenty of salted water, cover and simmer over gentle heat until tender, about 3 hours, adding a little water if necessary to keep covered. Drain and mix with the *tomatada*.

Serve as an accompaniment to fish or meat.

Grão com espinafres
(Chick Peas and Spinach)

An unusual combination of vegetables, but very tasty. It is generally served as an accompaniment to *bacalhau*, but is good also with other dishes.

Serves four

½ lb. chick peas   seasoning
1 lb. spinach   4 fl. oz. beef stock
1 large onion, sliced   3 tablespoons olive oil

Soak the chick peas for 24 hours.

The next day, wash the spinach well and put it in a saucepan in alternate layers with the chick peas and onion, seasoning each layer. Add the stock and sprinkle with the oil. Cover the pan and cook over gentle heat until the chick peas are tender, about 2–2½ hours. Add a little water if the mixture becomes too dry, but when the cooking is finished all the water should have been absorbed.

Abóbora carneira guisada com tomates
(Stewed Calabash with Tomatoes)

This national dish uses calabash, but any firm-fleshed squash or pumpkin may be used. It is primarily a vegetable dish, but the addition of ½ lb. chopped garlic or ham sausage will make a nourishing and tasty luncheon or supper dish.

Serves four

2 fl. oz. olive oil	seasoning
1 medium onion, finely sliced	1½ lb. flesh of squash, skin
1 sprig parsley, chopped	and seeds removed, cut into
1 medium tomato, skinned	small cubes
and chopped	

Heat the oil in a saucepan, add the onion and cook gently until limp and golden. Add the parsley and tomato, season, and cook gently for 5 minutes. Add the squash and simmer until tender, about 20 to 25 minutes.

Batatas estufadas à Portuguesa

(literally Stewed Potatoes; in reality boiled potatoes with a tomato sauce)

Serves four

1 lb. potatoes	1 tablespoon grated Parmesan
tomatada à Portuguesa (see	cheese
p. 89, but using ½ lb.	
tomatoes, 1 medium onion	
and 3 tablespoons olive oil)	

Scrub the potatoes, but do not peel, and cook them in boiling salted water until tender. Drain and, when cool enough, remove the skins and slice thickly. Place the slices in a buttered oven-proof dish, pour over the *tomatada* and sprinkle with the Parmesan cheese. Put in a moderate oven (350° F., gas 4) until heated through and lightly browned, about 5–10 minutes.

Favas frescas em salada
(Broad Bean Salad)

Serves four

1 lb. shelled broad beans	2 tablespoons olive oil
salt	1 clove garlic, crushed
ground black pepper	1 sprig parsley, chopped

Cook the beans in boiling salted water until tender. Drain and allow to get cold.

To make the dressing, mix the salt and pepper with the olive oil, add the garlic and finally the parsley.

Place the beans in a salad bowl, pour over the dressing and mix well.

Salade de feijão frade em frio
(Salad of Haricot Beans)

Serves four

1 lb. haricot beans	6 tablespoons olive oil
1 medium onion, chopped	seasoning
2 tablespoons white wine vinegar	1 sprig parsley, chopped

Soak the beans in water overnight. Drain and put them in a saucepan with plenty of salted water. Cover and cook over gentle heat until they are tender but firm, about 1 to 1½ hours.

Drain and allow to cool. Mix in the onion and a dressing made with the vinegar, oil and seasoning, and sprinkle with the parsley.

Salada de tomates
(Tomato Salad)

Serves four

1 lb. tomatoes, sliced	ground black pepper
1 large onion, sliced	1 tablespoon white wine vinegar
1 sprig coriander, chopped	3 tablespoons olive oil
salt	

Place the tomatoes, onion and coriander in a salad bowl.

Make the dressing in the usual way, i.e. mix the seasoning with the vinegar and add the oil.

Pour the dressing over the salad and mix well.

Tomatada à Portuguesa
(Portuguese Tomato Pulp)

4 tablespoons olive oil	1 clove garlic, crushed
1 large onion, sliced	1 sprig parsley, chopped
¾ lb. ripe tomatoes, skinned and chopped	seasoning

Heat the oil in a saucepan, add the onion and cook over gentle heat until limp and lightly golden. Add the tomatoes, garlic and parsley and simmer, uncovered, until the liquid has almost evaporated, about 20–30 minutes. Season.

Use as a sauce for eggs, meat or fish, as filling for an omelette or as a vegetable dish with chick peas (see *grão com tomatada*, p. 86).

Molho de azeda
(Sorrel Sauce)

For six servings

8 large leaves of sorrel	2 egg yolks, beaten
3 oz. butter	seasoning
1 tablespoon flour	

Remove and discard the stalks and tough ribs from the sorrel. Wash the leaves thoroughly, place them in a small saucepan with just the moisture that remains on them, cover and cook gently until tender, about 5 minutes. Drain and pass through a fine sieve.

Melt the butter in a saucepan, mix in the flour and cook for 2 minutes. Add the sorrel and the beaten egg yolks and cook over gentle heat until the mixture has slightly thickened. Season.

Serve as a sauce with dishes such as *lingua de vaca à Portuguesa* (see p. 62).

Cebolada à Portuguesa

(Onion Sauce or Stuffing)

This *cebolada* may be used as a filling for an omelette or served with fried or poached eggs as a supper dish. It is also very good as a sauce for fried fish, but in this case without the *presunto* or ham.

1¾ oz. butter	2 cloves garlic, crushed
2 large onions, sliced	1 sprig parsley, chopped
1 tablespoon white wine	seasoning
vinegar	3 oz. *presunto* (see p. 18) *or*
2 tablespoons tomato purée	lean ham, chopped

Melt the butter in a *frigideira* or frying pan, add the onions, and cook over gentle heat until limp. Mix the vinegar with the tomato purée and add to the onions together with the garlic, parsley and seasoning. Cover the pan and simmer until the mixture is softened and almost all the moisture has evaporated, about 20–25 minutes. About 10 minutes before the end of the cooking mix in the *presunto* or ham.

Arroz com grelos à Portuguesa

(Rice with Turnip Tops)

Turnip tops are much used as a vegetable, cooked very much in the same way as sprout tops. The recipe below, however, incorporates them with rice, making a rather more substantial dish. Sprout tops can be used instead.

Serves four

6 tablespoons olive oil	1 pint chicken stock
1 medium onion, sliced	seasoning
1 medium carrot, grated	¼ lb. tender parts of turnip
½ lb. round grain rice	tops

Heat 3 tablespoons of the olive oil in a saucepan, add the onion and carrot and cook until the onion is limp. Add the rice and cook gently for about 5 minutes, turning until all the grains are covered with oil. Add the stock, cover and cook over gentle heat until the rice is tender and all the liquid has disappeared, about 20–25 minutes. Season.

Meanwhile cook the turnip tops in boiling salted water until tender, about 5 minutes. Drain, squeezing out all the water, and chop.

Heat the rest of the olive oil in a small frying pan, add the turnip tops and cook over low heat for 15 minutes. Strain off any remaining oil and add the turnip tops to the mixture in the saucepan. Season if necessary and mix well.

Arroz com ervilhas à Ribatejana
(Rice with Peas from the Ribatejo)

Serves four

2 oz. butter	1 pint beef stock
12 oz. risotto rice washed and drained	12 oz. shelled peas
	seasoning

In a saucepan, melt 1½ oz. of the butter, add the rice and cook gently, turning frequently, for about 5 minutes. Add the stock, cover and cook gently until the rice is tender and all the liquid has disappeared, about 20 to 30 minutes.

Meanwhile cook the peas in salted water until tender, then drain. Add them to the rice, together with the remaining ½ oz. of butter, season and mix well.

Arroz c ervilhas em pudim à Alentejana
(Rice and Pea Pudding from the Alentejo)

A variation on *arroz com ervilhas à Ribatejana,* using eggs and *presunto* or ham and making a more substantial dish.

Serves four

arroz com ervilhas à Ribatejana (see above), using 8 oz. rice and 8 oz. shelled peas	½ oz. butter
	¼ lb. *presunto* (see p. 18) *or* ham, chopped
2 medium onions, sliced	4 eggs, beaten
	seasoning

Proceed as in the recipe for *arroz com ervilhas à Ribatejana*.

Meanwhile cook the onions gently in the butter until limp, and 10 minutes before the rice is cooked add them and the *presunto* or ham. When the mixture is finally cooked add the well-beaten eggs. Season to taste. Pour the mixture into a well-buttered oven-proof dish and cook in a hot oven (440° F., gas 7) until the eggs have just set, about 10 to 15 minutes.

Arroz de manteiga
(Buttered Rice)

Serves four

4 oz. butter	1 pint chicken stock
1 medium onion, sliced	seasoning
10 oz. risotto rice	

Melt 1 oz. of the butter in a saucepan, add the onion and cook gently until limp and golden. Add the rice, stirring well until all the grains are covered by the butter. Pour in the stock and add the rest of the butter. Season. Cover and cook over gentle heat until the rice is tender and all the moisture has been absorbed, about 30 minutes.

Puddings

Eggs, sugar and almonds are the main ingredients of Portuguese puddings, and what a delicious combination they make. Additions such as cinnamon, candied peel and lemon vary according to the region.

Quite a number of the recipes originated in the convents of earlier days, where the nuns had the time and the necessary ingredients to make these dishes.

Ovos moles, which can be eaten on its own or used as a filling, as in *torta de Viana*, is frequently encountered throughout Portugal. Perhaps the most subtle version is made in Aveiro, where it is sold in little barrels in the many confectioners' shops.

Pudim flan appears on many Portuguese menus; and, getting away from the usual egg and sugar combination, *arroz doce*, a cold rice and egg pudding, is very popular, and very good too.

In contrast with these rich concoctions, there are a number of dishes made from the fresh local fruits.

Ovos moles

Aveiro has been described as a little Venice. Quite a few places in the world have been so described, but in the case of Aveiro I think the description is apt. The town is intersected by a number of canals and on these travel gaily coloured boats. Even more like Venice are the red and white striped poles, placed at intervals along the canals, to which these boats are moored.

Aveiro is known as the birthplace of *ovos moles*, a delicious mixture of egg yolks, sugar and water which is made throughout Portugal. The first recipe I have given is the simple one used generally as a sauce or filling. The more elaborate one made in Aveiro is served by itself as a sweet.

8 oz. sugar	6 egg yolks
4 fl. oz. water	

Make a thin syrup by boiling the sugar in the water until it is dissolved. Allow to cool slightly. Beat the egg yolks and then slowly add the syrup, while continuing to beat. Return the mixture to the saucepan and cook gently, stirring constantly, until thickened, but do not allow to boil. Pour into a dish and use when cold.

Ovos moles d'Aveiro

Serves four

1 pint water	6 egg yolks
2 oz. rice	cinnamon
8 oz. sugar	

Bring the water to the boil in a saucepan, add the rice and cook for 15 minutes. Drain, reserve 4 fl. oz. of the water but discard the rice.

Put the sugar and the rice water into the saucepan and boil to make a thin syrup. Allow to cool slightly. Beat the egg yolks and then slowly add the syrup, while continuing to beat. Put the mixture into the saucepan and cook gently, stirring constantly, until thickened, but do not allow to boil. Pour into a serving dish and, when cold, sprinkle the top with cinnamon.

Doce de claras e ovos moles
(Egg White and Ovos Moles Sweet)

Serves four

4 egg whites	*ovos moles* (see p. 94), using
1 dessertspoon lemon juice	3 oz. sugar, 1½ fl. oz. water
3 oz. sugar	and 4 egg yolks

Beat the egg whites with the lemon juice and sugar until stiff. Put the mixture in tablespoonfuls into a fireproof dish, pour the *ovos moles* over and cook in a slow oven (250° F., gas ¼) until just firm, about 15 minutes.

This pudding may be eaten either hot or cold.

Pudim flan

Pudim flan is one of the most popular puddings in Portugal and is served throughout the country. Its name is slightly misleading: there is no pastry, so it is not a flan in the English sense. It can best be described as a crème caramel.

It is most frequently flavoured with a little vanilla essence, but this is sometimes varied by the substitution of melted chocolate, coffee or a liqueur. In the recipe below I have used coffee, as it blends very well with the rather burnt taste of the caramel.

Serves four

¾ lb. castor sugar	1 pint milk
4 eggs	1 tablespoon strong coffee *or*
4 egg yolks	coffee essence

Put 3 oz. of the sugar in a small saucepan and allow it to melt without stirring, then stir carefully until it is well browned. Pour into a warmed soufflé dish, rotating it slowly to cover the bottom of the dish.

In a large bowl lightly beat the rest of the sugar with the whole eggs and egg yolks. Bring the milk to the boil in a saucepan and gradually add it to the egg mixture, continuing to beat. Stir in the coffee.

Pour the mixture into the soufflé dish and cover the top with foil. Place in a baking tin and pour enough boiling water into the tin to reach half-way up the sides of the dish. Bake in a moderate oven (350° F., gas 4) until just set, about 1 hour, testing with a skewer which should come out clean.

Remove from the oven and cool. Chill and when ready to serve gently pass the blade of a knife round the edges and turn out.

Arroz doce à Portuguesa
(Portuguese Rice Sweet)

During the popular festival of São João in June the streets and squares of Alfama, the oldest part of Lisbon, are crowded with people. It is the gayest of crowds. The entertainment is completely spontaneous – there is singing and dancing, and there are stalls where you can buy all manner of things, from paper flowers and pots of a sweet-smelling plant called *manjericão* to cakes and sardines. The latter are grilled in the open over small braziers and you eat them with your fingers just as they are.

Outside most of the cafés and shops one sees displayed for sale small bowls of *arroz doce*, a rice sweet popular throughout Portugal. Usually the top is decorated with powdered cinnamon, and Portuguese cooks are adept in making designs, such as the cock, the national symbol, or a name, frequently Maria in honour of the Virgin Mary.

Serves six

a good pinch of salt	¼ lb. sugar
¼ lb. round-grained rice	3 egg yolks
1 pint milk	1 oz. butter
several pieces of lemon rind	powdered cinnamon for
1 stick cinnamon	decoration

Add the rice to a pan of boiling salted water and boil hard for 10 minutes. Meanwhile in another saucepan bring the milk to the boil with the lemon rind and stick of cinnamon. Drain the rice and add it to the milk. Allow it to cook gently for 5 minutes, then take it from the heat and remove the lemon rind and cinnamon. Stir in the sugar, beat the egg yolks and add them, together with the butter.

Replace the mixture over gentle heat and cook, stirring continuously, until it thickens slightly. Do not allow it to boil.

Pour into small individual bowls and sprinkle the tops with powdered cinnamon. Serve cold.

Leite creme
(Milk Sweet)

Serves four

5 oz. castor sugar	2 egg yolks
1 oz. cornflour	vanilla flavouring
¾ pint milk	granulated sugar

Mix the sugar and cornflour in a saucepan and cook over low heat, gradually adding the milk and stirring continuously. Bring to the boil and boil for 2 or 3 minutes. Remove from the heat. Beat the egg yolks with a little cold milk and add them to the mixture in the pan. Return the pan to gentle heat and cook until the mixture thickens slightly. Do not boil. Add vanilla flavouring to taste.

Pour into a heatproof serving dish, generously sprinkle the top with granulated sugar and brown under the grill.

Aletria doce
(Vermicelli Sweet)

Serves six

1¼ pints milk	8 oz. vermicelli
6 oz. castor sugar	3 egg yolks
1 oz. butter	ground cinnamon
grated rind of 1 lemon	

Bring the milk to the boil with the sugar, butter and grated lemon rind. Add the vermicelli and simmer until it has completely absorbed the milk. Beat the egg yolks and add to the mixture, stirring constantly. When the sweet reaches the desired consistency, pour into a serving dish and sprinkle with the cinnamon. Serve at once.

Sonhos
(Dreams)

A dessert of beignets served with a spiced syrup.

Makes about 12 *sonhos*

7 fl. oz. water	4 oz. self-raising flour
2 oz. butter	4 eggs
a pinch of salt	oil for frying

for the syrup

8 oz. sugar	1 stick cinnamon
¼ pint water	grated rind of 1 lemon

To make the syrup, put all the ingredients into a saucepan, bring to the boil, stirring until the sugar is dissolved, and boil for 3 minutes without stirring. Remove from the heat, take out the cinnamon and keep warm.

Bring the water, butter and salt to the boil in a saucepan, add the flour all at once and mix rapidly. Cook over gentle heat, beating continuously, until the mixture comes away from the sides of the pan. Remove from the heat and allow to cool slightly. Beat each egg separately into the mixture and then continue to beat for 15 minutes, until the mixture is quite smooth.

Put oil to a depth of half an inch in a shallow pan and bring to a moderate heat. Drop in dessertspoonfuls of the mixture, a few at a time, and cook gently, turning once, until they are puffed up and lightly browned. Remove and drain on absorbent paper. Arrange on a serving dish and pour the syrup over. Serve at once.

Farófias

Serves four

1¼ pints milk	4 eggs
grated rind of 1 lemon	6 oz. sugar
1 vanilla bean	powdered cinnamon

Heat the milk in a large pan with the lemon rind and vanilla bean. Separate the eggs and beat the whites until stiff. When the milk is simmering drop in large spoonfuls of the egg whites and cook gently, turning once, until just firm, about 4 minutes. Lift out with a perforated spoon, put to drain for a short time on absorbent paper and then place in a shallow dish.

Strain the milk, beat the egg yolks with the sugar until light and creamy, then gradually add the warm milk, beating continuously. Put in a pan and cook gently, stirring continually, until the mixture thickens slightly. Do not allow to boil. Cool and pour over the egg whites. Cover the dish and chill. Just before serving sprinkle with the cinnamon.

Papos d'anjo

Serves four

4 egg yolks	4 fl. oz. water
1 egg white	1 vanilla bean
½ lb. sugar	

Beat the egg yolks until creamy. Beat the egg white until stiff and fold into the yolks. Grease and flour some small shallow patty tins, about two inches in diameter. Spoon some of the mixture into each and cook in a hot oven (400° F., gas 7) for about 5 minutes, until it has just set. Turn out the *papos d'anjo* on to a wire rack and allow to cool slightly.

Put the sugar, water and vanilla bean in a saucepan, bring to the boil, stirring until the sugar is dissolved, and then boil hard, without stirring, for a few minutes, to make a syrup. Allow to cool.

Dip the *papos d'anjo* one by one in the syrup, place them on a dish and chill. Serve with the rest of the syrup poured over.

Barrigas de freira

Serves six

1 *pão de ló* (see p. 108)	1 teaspoon cocoa
10 oz. granulated sugar	3 whole eggs
3 fl. oz. water	3 egg yolks
grated rind of 1 lemon	1 oz. butter

Cut the *pão de ló* into six pieces and place them on a serving dish.

Bring the sugar, water, lemon rind and cocoa to the boil in a large frying pan and boil for one minute.

Meanwhile beat together the whole eggs and the yolks. Reduce the heat, keep the sugar mixture gently simmering and spoon the beaten eggs into it in six spoonfuls. They will spread a little. Put a little butter on the top of each. Do not over-cook, but remove them carefully from the syrup while still moist. Place them on the pieces of cake and cover with the syrup. Serve at once.

Mousse de chocolate Viriato

Serves six

4 oz. plain chocolate in tablet form	1 orange
1 oz. butter	5 eggs
	5 oz. castor sugar

Melt the chocolate and butter in a saucepan over low heat. Add the grated rind and the juice of an orange. When all is well mixed remove from the heat and add the beaten egg yolks one at a time, stirring continuously.

Beat the egg whites until stiff. Fold in the sugar and continue to beat for a further few seconds, until well blended. Add the chocolate mixture and stir sufficiently to mix in all the ingredients.

Pour the mousse into a glass dish or individual glasses and chill.

Pudim de laranja
(Orange Pudding)

Serves four

3 eggs	$\frac{3}{4}$ lb. castor sugar
7 egg yolks	juice of 3 oranges

In a large bowl, beat all the ingredients together until light and well mixed, about 10 minutes. Leave for $\frac{1}{2}$ an hour to allow the bubbles to subside.

Grease a large soufflé dish and pour in the mixture. Place the dish in a tin with hot water reaching half-way up the sides of the dish.

Cook in a slow oven (325° F., gas 3) for about one hour, until the mixture is just firm throughout. Cool before serving.

Pudim de ananás
(Pineapple Pudding)

When making Portuguese sweets, which so often use mainly or only the yolks of eggs, one accumulates a large number of whites. This pudding gives an opportunity to use some of them up.

Serves four

½ oz. gelatine	1 oz. sugar
1 tablespoon lemon juice	3 egg whites
2 tablespoons cold water	2 tablespoons Kirsch
8 oz. fresh pineapple (*or*	4 fl. oz. double cream
tinned, drained of juice)	½ teaspoon vanilla essence

Put the gelatine in a saucepan with the lemon juice and water and allow to stand for 5 minutes; then dissolve over gentle heat. Chop the pineapple finely, add it with the sugar and simmer, stirring, until the sugar has dissolved. Do not allow to boil.

Remove from the heat and cool. When the mixture is cold, but not set, fold in the egg whites, stiffly beaten, and the Kirsch. Pour into a mould and chill.

Turn out on to a dish to serve. Whip the cream, add the vanilla essence, and hand round separately.

Ananás com vinho do porto
(Pineapple with Port Wine)

This sweet is served throughout Portugal.

1 slice pineapple per person,	granulated sugar
peeled and cored	port

Sprinkle the slices of pineapple with granulated sugar and then with port. Chill and serve.

Salada de frutas
(Fruit Salad)

Serves four to six

1½ lb. fresh fruits	1 wineglass port
4 oz. raisins	juice of 1 orange
5 oz. sugar	juice of half a lemon

Put the prepared fruit and raisins in a bowl and sprinkle with the sugar. Add the port and fruit juices and mix gently. Chill thoroughly before serving.

Torta de Viana

This is one of those 'melt in the mouth' sweets. It resembles our swiss roll, but has more eggs and less flour. Filled with *ovos moles*, it seems to ooze with goodness.

5 eggs	icing sugar
4 oz. sugar	*ovos moles* (see p. 94, but
1 tablespoon self-raising flour	using half quantities)

Separate the egg yolks and whites. Beat the yolks and the sugar until light and creamy and gradually add the flour. Whip the egg whites until dry and fold into the egg and sugar mixture.

Grease a shallow swiss-roll tin. Line with greaseproof paper and grease this very well. Pour in the mixture and cook in a hot oven (450° F., gas 8) until risen and just firm, about 10 minutes.

Sprinkle another sheet of greaseproof paper with sieved icing sugar and turn the cake out on to this. Cover with *ovos moles* and quickly roll up with the aid of the paper.

Charcada

The basic recipe has just a sprinkling of cinnamon for the flavouring. However, the one we had in Lisbon had raisins and orange juice added, and this is the recipe I have given below.

Serves four

1 slice white bread, without the crust	½ lb. castor sugar
2 fl. oz. milk	4 fl. oz. water
2 oz. raisins	3 egg yolks
juice of ½ an orange	2 oz. ground almonds

Break up the bread into very small pieces and soak in the milk. Drain and squeeze out.

Soak the raisins in the orange juice until softened. Then drain, reserving the juice.

Put the sugar and water into a saucepan. Bring to the boil over a moderate heat and boil gently, stirring continuously, until the sugar is dissolved. Remove from the heat and cool. Beat the egg yolks and add them to the sugar solution together with the ground almonds, bread and raisins. Reheat the mixture and cook gently until it has thickened, about 10 minutes. Remove from the heat and stir in the orange juice.

Pour into individual small bowls and chill.

Trouxas de ovos
(Egg Bundles)

These little egg bundles covered with a syrup are a speciality of Caldas de Rainha in Estramadura. They may be a little difficult to make at first, but the result is well worth all the trouble. The recipe I was given uses a little coconut for a filling, which is a variation from the usual.

Serves four

12 oz. sugar	1 egg white
6 fl. oz. water	desiccated coconut
6 egg yolks	

Put the sugar and water into a small frying pan, bring to the boil and boil until the temperature of the syrup reaches 220°F. Reduce the heat but keep simmering.

With the aid of a fork, pass the egg yolks gently through a wire sieve into a bowl. Beat the egg white and slowly add to the yolks. Put some of the egg mixture into an egg cup and pour gently into

the syrup. Cook until just set, pressing under the syrup for a short
time to cook the top. Lift out with a perforated slice and put on a
plate. Trim the edges, putting the pieces in the middle together
with a little of the coconut, roll up and place in a serving dish.
Repeat the operation until all the egg mixture is used. Pour over a
little of the syrup. Serve cold.

Cakes, Sweetmeats and Conserves

The Portuguese cakes and sweets are, like their puddings, very sweet and rich. The principal ingredients are eggs, sugar and almonds. Some of the regional specialities do use other ingredients as well, such as cheese in the tarts of Sintra and Evora and dried beans in those of Torres Vedras. One or two of the cakes resemble the traditional ones of other countries, such as the Twelfth Night cake, *bolo rei*; but most could only have one country of origin, Portugal.

No notes on Portuguese sweetmeats would be complete without special reference to those of the Algarve, that region of abundance of almonds and figs. The imagination and ingenuity which go into their making have to be seen to be believed. Dried figs and finely ground almonds (it is not unusual to pass them seven times through a sieve) are cleverly moulded into realistic shapes of birds, animals and baskets of fruit and flowers. Faro, the capital of the Algarve, is probably the principal centre for these sweetmeats and a shop-gazing walk through the narrow streets is a mouth-watering experience.

Bolo rei
(King's Cake)

Bolo rei is the cake which, like the *galette du roi* of France, is eaten on Twelfth Night. It is baked in circles, said to represent the crowns of the three wise men.

Portuguese recipes usually cater for larger numbers than we cook for, and the recipe I was given was enough to make two large 'crowns'. I have therefore halved the ingredients to make one large 'crown'.

¼ oz. fresh yeast
11 oz. flour, sieved
2 tablespoons milk
2 eggs, beaten
¼ teaspoon salt
2 oz. sugar
2 oz. melted butter
1½ oz. raisins

1½ oz. glacé cherries, chopped
1½ oz. almonds, chopped
1½ oz. pine kernels, chopped
1 egg yolk, beaten
granulated sugar and chopped
    crystallized fruit and nuts
    for decoration

Dissolve the yeast in a dessertspoon of tepid water and, in a warm bowl, mix it with 2 oz. of the flour and enough tepid water to make a dough. Cover with a cloth and leave in a warm place for 20 minutes.

Warm the milk and add it to the dough with the rest of the flour, the eggs, salt and sugar. Beat the mixture, gradually adding the butter. Turn out on to a floured board and knead until smooth, about 15 minutes. Put into a large bowl, cover with a cloth and leave in a warm place to rise until doubled in bulk, about 2–3 hours.

Add the raisins, cherries and nuts. Knead and allow to stand for 10 minutes. Grease a large tin, form the dough into a circle on it and place a jam-jar in the middle to keep it open while it rises. Leave to rise in a warm place for about an hour. Gently brush the top with the beaten egg yolk and decorate it with the nuts, crystallized fruit and sugar. Bake in a moderate oven (350° F., gas 4) until firm and golden, about 20–25 minutes. Remove from the oven, place on a wire rack and cool.

Bolo podre de Estremoz

A spiced honey cake from Estremoz in the Alentejo region.

4 large eggs
3½ oz. castor sugar
6 fl. oz. olive oil
6 fl. oz. honey

grated rind of 2 oranges
2 tablespoons brandy
½ lb. self-raising flour
2 teaspoons mixed spice

Separate the yolks and whites of the eggs. Beat the yolks with the sugar. Beat in the olive oil little by little, then the honey, the grated orange rind and the brandy. Sieve the flour and spice and beat into the batter. Whip the egg whites until stiff but not dry, and gently fold into the batter.

Pour the mixture into a greased round tin with a removable bottom. Bake in a slow oven (325° F., gas 3) for about 1 hour, until the cake top is firm, and a skewer when it is inserted comes out clean. Leave in the tin until cool. Remove and place on a wire rack.

This cake improves with keeping.

Bolo Algarvio
(Algarve Cake)

½ lb. castor sugar
¼ pint water
½ lb. ground almonds
4 egg yolks

2 egg whites
2 oz. butter
1 oz. plain flour
1 teaspoon ground cinnamon

Put the sugar and the water in a saucepan. Bring to the boil, stirring until the sugar is dissolved, and continue to boil until the temperature reaches 220° F. Remove from the heat and add the ground almonds, the egg yolks and whites well beaten, the butter, flour and cinnamon. Return to gentle heat and cook, stirring continuously, until the mixture forms a paste.

Take off the heat and allow to cool, then put the mixture into a shallow baking tray which has been previously greased and floured.

Cook in a slow oven (325° F., gas 3) until lightly browned, about 20 minutes. Allow to get cold, then cut into large slices and powder them with cinnamon and sugar.

Bolo de abade
(Abbot's Cake)

6 egg yolks	1 oz. self-raising flour
½ lb. sugar	½ lb. ground almonds
4 egg whites	

Beat the yolks and sugar together well, add the whites and continue to beat for 10 minutes. Fold in the flour and the ground almonds. Butter an 8-inch cake tin, line with greaseproof paper and butter the paper thoroughly. Pour in the mixture and bake in a hot oven (450° F., gas 8), until a skewer inserted in the centre comes out clean, about 45 minutes. Cover with foil if the top is becoming too brown.

Pão de ló
(Portuguese Sponge Cake)

This recipe is for a sponge cake with a difference: it is Portuguese and consequently is rich in eggs and sugar. Served in the paper in which it was cooked, it is light and slightly moist in the centre.

Some of the regional versions use a quantity of eggs which would surprise even Mrs Beeton. The *pão de ló de Peniche* has 24 egg yolks and 12 whites, and the richest of all, the *pão de ló de Alfeizerão*, uses 35 yolks and 9 whole eggs; a little shattering for a frugally minded cook.

The recipe below is for a simple *pão de ló* and uses 8 eggs.

8 eggs	1 teaspoon vanilla essence
¼ lb. sugar	2 oz. self-raising flour

Grease two cake tins and line with greaseproof paper. The circles of paper should be large enough to come up the sides of the tins so that they can be used to lift out the cakes when they are cooked. Grease the paper well.

Separate the eggs. Beat the whites until dry, fold in 2 oz. of the sugar and continue to beat until stiff. In another bowl beat the yolks with the rest of the sugar until light and creamy. Add the essence. Sieve the flour and add it also to the mixture. Finally fold in the egg whites.

Pour the mixture into the two tins and cook in a slow oven (325° F., gas 3) until the top of the cake is just golden and it is set round the edge but not in the centre (about 20 minutes).

Remove from the oven, lift carefully out of the tins with the paper and cool on a wire rack.

Pastéis de feijão
(Bean Tartlets)

Torres Vedras is an area of small undulating hills, famous during the Peninsular War campaigns. It is the region where these little tarts are a speciality. They are filled with a mixture of almonds and finely sieved dried beans. This may seem a curious filling for a sweet tart, but the beans give a nutty flavour which is very pleasant.

Makes about 18 tartlets

2 oz. dried haricot beans	8 oz. flour
8 oz. sugar	pinch of salt
4 fl. oz. water	3 oz. butter
4 tablespoons ground almonds	3 oz. lard
6 egg yolks	icing sugar

Soak the beans overnight. Cook with plenty of water in a covered saucepan over gentle heat until tender, about 40 minutes. Drain and sieve.

Put the sugar and the water in a saucepan, bring to the boil, stirring until the sugar is dissolved, and boil for 3 minutes. Remove from the heat and add the bean purée. Cook gently for 3–4 minutes, then stir in the ground almonds. When the mixture just begins to bubble, remove from the heat and allow to cool. Beat the egg yolks and add to the mixture. Return to the heat and cook gently, stirring continuously, until it thickens slightly, but do not allow to boil. Remove from the heat and allow to cool.

Meanwhile sieve the flour and salt into a bowl, rub in the fats until the mixture resembles fine breadcrumbs and add enough cold water to make a soft dough. Roll on a floured board and cut out three-inch circles and with them line some greased tartlet tins.

Fill the pastry cases with the mixture, sprinkle with sieved icing sugar and bake in a hot oven (400° F., gas 7) until cooked, about 15–20 minutes.

Lérias

Amarante in the Douro is famous for its cakes. There are many kinds, all different shapes and sizes. São Gonçalo, the patron saint of marriages, is buried in Amarante, and during the June and September festivals of the town, cakes shaped like a phallus are given by the young men to their girls, a relic of a fertility custom of many centuries past.

The Lérias given below are small cakes full of almonds and covered with a glaze.

10 oz. ground almonds	12 oz. icing sugar
10 oz. castor sugar	3 fl. oz. milk
2 oz. flour	2 tablespoons lemon juice
2 fl. oz. tepid water	

Mix the ground almonds, castor sugar and flour with the tepid water and knead the mixture. With floured hands, break off small quantities and make into rolls. Place these on a greased, floured tin, flattening them slightly with the hand. Bake in a moderate oven (350° F., gas 4) until firm and very slightly golden, about 10 minutes.

Meanwhile make a glaze by sieving the icing sugar into a bowl and mixing in the milk and lemon juice.

Remove the cakes from the oven and, while still warm, carefully dip them into the glaze, then put them on a wire rack to cool and dry.

Cristas de galo

(Cockscombs – cakes from Vila Real)

for the pastry

1 lb. self-raising flour	4 oz. butter
pinch of salt	cold water
4 oz. lard	

for the filling

8 oz. sugar	1 green apple, grated with the
2 fl. oz. water	peel
1 oz. lard	6 egg yolks, beaten
2 oz. flaked almonds	½ teaspoon ground cinnamon

Pastry

Sift the flour and salt into a bowl. Break up the lard and butter and rub them into the flour until the mixture resembles fine bread-crumbs. Add enough water to bind. Roll out very thinly.

Filling

Boil the sugar in the water until it is dissolved. Remove from the heat. Cut up the lard and add it together with the almonds and the apple. After the mixture has cooled, gradually add the egg yolks and the cinnamon, stirring constantly. Return to the heat and cook gently, stirring continuously, until slightly thickened. Allow to cool.

Cut circles of the pastry and in each place a spoonful of the filling. Moisten the edges of the pastry and join together in the shape of a cockscomb. Bake in a hot oven (450° F., gas 8) until lightly browned, about 15 minutes. Cool on a wire rack.

They are best eaten while still warm.

Queijadas de Sintra

(Sintra Cheesecakes)

Sintra has been known and loved by people from this country for many years now. Perhaps it was Byron who started the fashion, when he lived there for a time. Surrounded by wooded hills, it is very sheltered, and the vegetation is luxuriant and almost sub-tropical. The gardens of Montserrate, built by an Englishman on the outskirts of the town, contain, besides a profusion of beautiful and sometimes rare shrubs and trees, a world famous collection of ferns. The central square of the town is dominated by the Moorish-style palace, with peculiar oast-house shaped kitchen chimneys.

After visiting the gardens and the palace it is pleasant to go into one of the small confectioner's shops and taste some of these delectable little cheesecakes, a speciality of the town. The recipe

I was given specified ewes' cheese, but any kind of curd cheese will do.

for the pastry

4 oz. flour	pinch of salt	2 oz. butter

for the filling

12 oz. curd cheese, unsalted	1 oz. desiccated coconut
3 egg yolks, beaten	1 oz. ground almonds
8 oz. sugar	pinch of cinnamon
½ oz. flour	

Pastry

Sieve the flour and salt, then add the butter, cut into small pieces, and blend together until the mixture resembles breadcrumbs. Add enough cold water to make a soft dough. Roll out very thinly and cut into four-inch rounds. Make four symmetrical one-inch cuts in the edge of each round and turn up the four outer pieces to form the sides of a box.

Filling

Press the cheese through a sieve and mix with the beaten egg yolks and the sugar. Add the flour, coconut, ground almonds and cinnamon and mix well.

Spoon the filling into the pastry boxes and bake in a hot oven (400° F., gas 7) until the pastry is cooked and the tops are golden, about 15 minutes. Cool on a wire rack.

Touchinho do céu
(Food from Heaven)

4 oz. sugar	4 egg yolks
1 fl. oz. water	granulated sugar
5 oz. ground almonds	

Boil the sugar in the water until it is dissolved. Stir in the almonds and cook over moderate heat for 5 minutes. Cool, then slowly add the well-beaten egg yolks and cook gently, stirring continuously, until thickened; but do not allow to boil. Well grease a flan tin with a removable base. Turn the mixture into this and sprinkle the top with granulated sugar. Bake in a hot oven (400° F., gas 7) until just set, about 8 minutes. Cool, then remove from the tin.

Fios de ovos
(Egg Threads)

These are used for cake decoration and also as one of the ingredients of the Algarve sweetmeats Dom Rodrigos.

To make them egg yolks are dropped in a thin stream into boiling syrup. The nuns who invented the recipe long ago used for the purpose a half egg shell with a small hole in the bottom. Nowdays in Portugal you can buy a special funnel, but I have used the original method.

6 egg yolks	1 lb. granulated sugar
1 egg white	8 fl. oz. water

With the aid of a fork, gently pass the egg yolks and white through a sieve into a small bowl. In a large frying pan, bring the sugar and water to the boil, stirring until the sugar is dissolved, and continue to boil until the syrup reaches 220° F.

Make a small hole in the bottom of a half egg shell. Pour some of the egg into the shell and drop it in a thin stream into the boiling syrup, using a circular motion so that it forms threads resembling knitting wool. Cook until just set and then remove with a perforated slice and place in a sieve. With hands dipped in cold water, separate the threads and lay them on a wire rack to drain.

Repeat the operation until all the egg is used, keeping the syrup boiling and adding water as necessary from time to time to keep it at its initial concentration.

Dom Rodrigos

These Algarve sweetmeats are attractive to look at in their little beribboned packets and delicious to eat.

ovos moles (half quantity in recipe, p. 94)	2 oz. ground almonds
	syrup from *fios de ovos*
fios de ovos (see above)	foil and ribbon for wrapping

Mix the ground almonds into the *ovos moles*.

Mould the *fios de ovos* into flattish discs about 3 inches across and place a teaspoon of *ovos moles* in the centre of each. Cut a 5-inch square of foil for each portion. Fill a large frying pan with the syrup to a depth of ¼ inch, bring to the boil, boil until the syrup is golden and then keep boiling over moderate heat.

Carefully put a few of the *fios de ovos* portions into the boiling syrup, and with the aid of two knives wrap the *fios de ovos* round the *ovos moles*. Cook until lightly browned, about 2 minutes, remove with a perforated slice and place on the squares of foil. Repeat until all the portions are used. When set and cold draw up the sides of the foil and fasten with ribbon.

Morgado de figos do Algarve
(Fig Sweetmeat from the Algarve)

½ lb. dried figs	2 oz. powdered chocolate
½ lb. sugar	½ teaspoon ground cinnamon
4 fl. oz. water	grated rind of 1 lemon
½ lb. ground almonds	castor sugar for decoration

Pass the figs through a fine mincer.

In a saucepan bring the sugar and water to the boil, stirring until the sugar has dissolved. Continue to boil until the solution reaches 220°F.

Remove from the heat and add the rest of the ingredients. Return to the heat and cook gently until the mixture comes away cleanly from the sides of the pan.

Remove from the heat and allow to cool. When cool, spread evenly over the bottom of a shallow tin, sprinkle with castor sugar and cut into 2-inch squares.

Marmelada de marmelos
(Quince Cheese)

Quince *marmelada* is probably the most popular conserve in Portugal. I remember it served at breakfast time, cut into pink cubes rather like Turkish Delight, and eaten with delicious crisp white bread and rolls.

The bread of Portugal is good too. There is the maize bread or *broa*, more often found in the country districts, especially in the Alentejo where it is usually served with soup, for example *açorda*

Alentejana (see p. 26). Then there is the white wheaten bread which always has the flavour and texture of home-made bread.

One year we rented, in the Algarve, a flat which was built over the local bakery. Late each night we heard sounds of great activity coming from below – not disturbingly so, but enough to arouse our curiosity. So one evening returning late to the flat we went first of all below into the bakery. The baker and his assistant, glistening in the heat, in their shirt sleeves and wearing long white aprons and white skull caps were busy kneading large mounds of dough. Behind them were two brick ovens in which were burning bundles of brushwood, later to be raked out to give place to the dough. The whole scene was sadly reminiscent of days gone by when all bread was worked and baked in this way. I know that nowadays it might be said that this method is not economic, but I still think it makes the best bread.

2 lb quinces, peeled and cored	rind of 1 lemon
2¼ lb. granulated sugar	½ stick of cinnamon

Cut the quinces into small pieces and put in a pan with water almost to cover. Bring to the boil and simmer until pulped. Pass the pulp through a fine sieve (or liquidize).

Put the sugar in a pan with 4 fl. oz. of water and boil, stirring continuously, until the sugar is dissolved and the syrup begins to bubble. Add the quince pulp with the lemon rind and the cinnamon. Boil for a short time until the mixture begins to thicken, stirring all the time.

Remove from the heat and take out the lemon rind and cinnamon. Pot and cover immediately.

Bagulhada

A delicious conserve from the Alentejo region made of grapes, quince and nuts.

2 lb. black grapes	¼ lb. quince, peeled and cored
4 fl. oz. water	3 oz. nuts, chopped
1 lb. sugar	

Stone the grapes and put them in a pan with the water. Cover and simmer for 30 minutes. Add the sugar and the quinces, cut into small pieces, and stir until the sugar is dissolved, then boil the mixture until it gels.

Remove from the heat and stir in the nuts. Pot and cover immediately.

Sangria

To conclude, I thought it would be appropriate to give a recipe for a Portuguese drink.

1 litre red wine	1 small bottle soda water
1 glass brandy	fresh fruit, particularly
1 glass port	oranges, and strawberries
1 small bottle lemonade	when available

Mix all the ingredients in a large bowl and chill.

Index

Penguinews *and*
Penguins in Print

Every month we issue an illustrated magazine, *Penguinews*.
It's a lively guide to all the latest Penguins, Pelicans
and Puffins, and always contains an article on a
major Penguin author, plus other features of contemporary
interest.

Penguinews is supplemented by *Penguins in Print*, a
complete list of all the available Penguin titles – there are
now over four thousand!

Why not write for a free copy of this month's *Penguinews*?
And if you'd like both publications sent for a year, just
send us a cheque or a postal order for 30p (if you live in
the United Kingdom) or 60p (if you live elsewhere),
and we'll put you on our mailing list.

Dept EP, Penguin Books Ltd,
Harmondsworth, Middlesex

Note: *Penguinews* and *Penguins in Print*
are not available in the U.S.A. or Canada

Mediterranean Seafood

Alan Davidson

'What fish is it? Do we have something like it at home?'

Mediterranean seafood can be as baffling as it is fascinating, and this intriguing survey has been specially designed to cast light on the subject. In a scholarly and amusing style, and with the help of illustrations, Alan Davidson has catalogued the edible marine life of the Mediterranean and labelled it in several languages. British and American readers will find that the 200 recipes are skilfully presented so as to show how easily the native flavour of Mediterranean seafood can be brought into distant homes.

Arranging the dishes country by country, from the *Suquillo de Pescadores* of Spain and the famous *Anchoïade* and *Bouillabaisse* of Provençal France to the Greek *Ochtapódi Krassáto* – octopus cooked in red wine – the author includes also rarer recipes from such places as Istanbul, Alexandria and Bizerta. Alan Davidson possesses the quixotic charm of the true enthusiast and his practical directions are enlivened with touches which will induce interest and nostalgia in those who know the Mediterranean.

'Mr Davidson has a gift for conveying memorable information in a way so effortless that his book makes lively reading for its own sake' – Elizabeth David reviewing an earlier version in the *Spectator*.

Italian Food

Elizabeth David

Exploding once and for all the myth that Italians live
entirely on minestrone, spaghetti, and veal escalopes, this
exciting book demonstrates the enormous and colourful
variety of Italy's regional cooking. Listing well over four
hundred dishes, clearly described and helpfully
classified, the author of *A Book of Mediterranean Food*
and *French Country Cooking* also enumerates the various
herbs and spices required in many of them, sensibly
explaining where they may be bought, and there are useful
chapters on Italian wines and cheeses. The result is an
extremely readable guide to eating out in Italy which
is also a practical text-book for reproducing the best of
Italian food in your own kitchen.

Also available by Elizabeth David

Mediterranean Food

French Country Cooking

French Provincial Cooking

Summer Cooking

English Cooking, Ancient and Modern 1: Spices, Salt,
  and Aromatics in the English Kitchen

Penguin Cordon Bleu Cookery

Rosemary Hume and Muriel Downes

The term 'Cordon Bleu' has come to be accepted as the hallmark of culinary perfection – the very highest standard of European cooking with a French accent. This new Penguin cookery book, prepared by the co-principals of the English Cordon Bleu School, needs little other recommendation.

It is enough to say that it is written for people who like good food, with all that this means. The recipes for all kinds of dishes are clear and detailed, and the authors continually stress the importance of presentation – of colour, shape, and garnish. Equally they give the technical reasons for the methods they suggest, knowing that so much careless cooking is the result of an imperfect understanding.

With this handbook in the kitchen, and herself – at least, in one cunning series of recipes – in the sitting-room, no woman need be frightened of entertaining the most exacting *gourmets*.

The SHELTER Cookery Book

A collection of recipes from famous people

You may know a better recipe book than this. You'll never find one with more distinguished authors.

Just look at the Contents List. Here are the Prime Minister and the Archbishop of Canterbury crossing spoons with a bevy of bishops and actresses; Mary Wilson and Barbara Castle mixing it with Max Bygraves and Terry Wogan; Maître Chefs (not to mention Elizabeth David) cutting capers with a hundred stars of radio, film and TV, of pitch, page, pulpit, platform and palette.

And all for SHELTER.

Probably no other cause could mount such a glittering charity show for SHELTER is now rehousing people in Britain at the rate of ten families a day. By SHELTER's calculation there are still a million families in need of homes . . . and that calls for funds.

What better method of raising them than a kitchen frolic, in which Jeremy Thorpe forgoes his rights and the Earl of Harewood his royalties, all for the cause?

Just read the Contents List again. Surely you're not going to have it said you can't do as well as that lot. So buy a copy and contribute your mite.